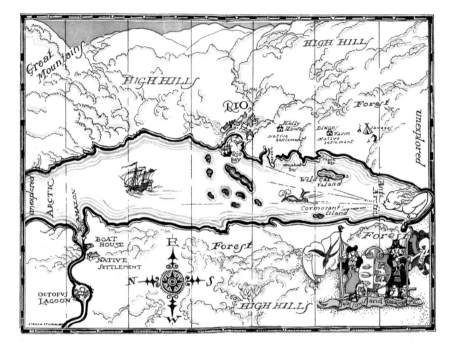

WRITING BRITAIN

WASTELANDS TO WONDERLANDS

Arthur Rackham

WRITING BRITAIN

WASTELANDS TO WONDERLANDS

Christina Hardyment

BRITISH LIBRARY

CONTENTS

OPPOSITE
First held in 1133,
Bartholomew Fair,
which took place every
August near Smithfield,
was London's longest
running piece of street
theatre. Engraving by
Rudolf Ackerman from
an original by Thomas
Rowlandson and
Auguste Charles Pugin,
published in William
Pyne's *Microcosm of
London* (1808–10).

GREAT BRI TAINE

By
Michaell Drayton
Esqr.

LOOK, STRANGER,
ON THIS ISLAND NOW

Britain is a country of dramatic contrasts: rural wonderlands and barren wastes, serene seascapes and inner city badlands, of picturesque lakes and mountains and monotonous suburbs. From the time that quills first etched words on parchment to today's hi-tech interactive literary media, writers have been intensely aware of the settings of their works, and have altered the way their readers experience them. Heathcliff and Cathy will always inhabit the moors above Haworth; the Swallows and the Amazons tack endlessly across their 'Lake in the North'. Matthew Arnold's 'Dover Beach', and Alice Oswald's *Dart* have given unforgettable new identities to their settings.

This book is a companion and complement to the 'Writing Britain: Wastelands to Wonderlands' exhibition at the British Library in May–September 2012. Ranging across nine centuries, it uses many of the literary treasures of the Library to illustrate writers' interpretations of place, from Chaucer's jocular presentation of pilgrims journeying from London to Canterbury to *Crash*, J.G. Ballard's fantastical take on London's suburban hinterland. It tells of rural dreams of Arcadia and odes to romantically gothic landscapes, of toiling farmers and the lowering threat of dark satanic mills. It moves from the seaside to the river bank, and into densely populated cityscapes that can be both threateningly dangerous and culturally vibrant. Finally it looks at the edgelands: suburbs where horrors can lurk in quiet bungalows on Wimbledon Common, and unofficial in-between places that provide harassed moderns with a way of getting back to lost roots.

It is full of famous names: Geoffrey Chaucer and Wordsworth, Jane Austen and Thomas Hardy, Emily Brontë and Robert Louis Stevenson, John Betjeman and Evelyn Waugh, W.H. Auden and Sylvia Plath, J.G. Ballard and Carol Ann Duffy, Iain Sinclair and Richard Mabey. But it is also a galaxy of many lesser-known talents who will hopefully provide the adventurous and curious with plenty of ideas for future reading, for example, 'Gypsy Sculler' John Taylor's seventeenth-century river poetry, Lady Morgan's romantic *The Wild Irish Girl*, and Richard Marsh's horrific tale of *The Beetle*.

For me the book that best sums up 'Writing Britain' is Michael Drayton's *Poly-Olbion*, a gloriously ambitious 16,000-line gazetteer of England and Wales, which was published in 1612. It was written in rhyming couplets and touched on history and geography, folk traditions and science, myth and magic. In the frontispiece, Britannia, flanked by home-grown heroes and draped in a map displaying her wonders, gazes out at the reader with twinkling eyes. In her arms is a cornucopia, a splendid symbol of the abundant riches that can be found once we begin to delve into the works of British writers old and new, male and female, famous and forgotten.

OPPOSITE
The frontispiece of Michael Drayton's *Poly-Olbion* (1612) showing Britannia clad in a cloak decorated with rivers and cities, and flanked by Hengest and William of Normandy.

RURAL DREAMS

Legends and the Land

The rural dream has been an enduring one. Spun by jaded courtiers under the first Queen Elizabeth, and re-imagined by country-born city-dwellers nostalgic for childhood, it is still escaped into by the nation when it tunes in to Radio 4's *The Archers* or strides out across a National Park. Its roots lie in the legends that have laced the history of Britain from earliest times. These tales of Eden and Albion have shape-shifted through the centuries to suit the times in which they are told and the mood of the people – minstrels, antiquaries, poets and novelists – who relate them. The rural dream has been slanted to teach the virtues of feudal obedience, the value of inter-dependent community, a sense of the continuity of past and present.

CHAPTER OPENER
Detail of a painting of the Gloucestershire village of Slad, *c*.1926, by Laurie Lee, author of *Cider with Rosie*.

OPPOSITE
Lady Charlotte Guest's translation of the ancient Welsh legends known as the Mabinogion proved an immensely popular addition to the canon of Arthurian legends, and were often retold for children. Illustration from *The Boy's Mabinogion* (1881), edited by Sidney Lanier.

In rejecting the dominance of the intellectual and the mechanical, it celebrates honest toil, sensory experience and simplicity. Inevitably conservative, in the best sense of the word, the dream grew to its greatest intensity first during the dizzyingly fast industrialisation of the nineteenth century and again during two World Wars, in response to the threat posed to Britain's traditional identity. Most recently it has been reinvented in the literature of the environmental movement.

Legends that originated deep in what medieval writers called 'time out of mind' have proved enduring rural touchstones. They survived the arrival of the Romans, Anglo-Saxons and Danes, and the country's conversion to Christianity, passed down first by word of mouth, in stories told around winter firesides, then transcribed by monks. After the Conquest of 1066 Norman kings looked to the ancient past for justification of their rule in England. The bones of King Arthur were 'discovered' at Glastonbury during the twelfth-century reign of Henry II, and the potent chivalric myth of his knights' courage and loyalty was told and retold in halls and solars – first in medieval French, then in Old English rhyme.

The ancient Welsh legends of heroes only became generally known in the nineteenth century, when they were translated into English, in several volumes, by Lady Charlotte Guest (1812–94). Married to the owner of a Merthyr Tydfil iron foundry, Guest gave the collection the generic name of *Mabinogion* (derived from an early Welsh word for tales). Full of fantasy and magic, giants and snow-white steeds, clever women and stalwart men, they are set for the main part on the western coasts of South and North Wales, but mountains, lakes and forests also feature. Several refer to King Arthur and Merlin, and 'Bran the Blessed' has connections with the ailing Fisher King of the Grail legend.

Arthurian myth achieved its finest form in the supple and colourful everyday prose of Sir Thomas Malory (c.1400–71), who promised that Arthur, Britain's 'once and future king', would return whenever Albion needed to be saved. Malory rooted his version of the story in places his countrymen would recognise: Tintagel (where his uncle had been Constable), Winchester (where a Round Table said to have been King Arthur's was on show, as it still is), Avebury and Glastonbury. Even London played its part, with Lancelot fording the Thames on a horse by Westminster. *The Birth, Life and Acts of King Arthur, of his noble Knights of the Round Table, their marvellous Enquests and Adventures, th'Achieving of the Sangreal, and in the end the dolorous Death and Departing out of the World of them All* (which he completed in 1469) was so popular in its day that it became one of the earliest books published by William Caxton, England's first printer. The work appeared in print in 1485, just in time for the accession of

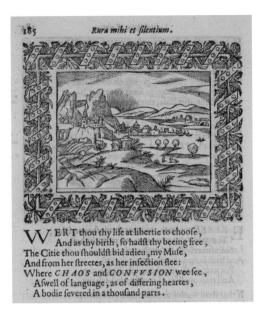

ABOVE
Escaping from urban stresses into rural peace is as old as cities. Henry Peacham's emblematic illustration and poem 'Rura Mihi et Silentium' from *Minerva Britanna* deplores the 'chaos and confusion' of court and city (*Minerva Britanna*, 1612).

the Tudors, who valued its Welsh associations in support of their own claim to the throne.

Intricately connected with Arthurian myths are those of the Green Man, a Celtic archetype whose face still peers from gargoyles and roof bosses in ancient churches. The most famous Green Man in literature is a 'hoodie' in Lincoln green whose supposed home now shifts between South Yorkshire and Sherwood Forest in Nottinghamshire. The first ballads of Robin Hood date from the fourteenth century. They tell of a folk hero, an outlawed yeoman who preferred freedom to conformity; the champion of women and the poor, he ceaselessly played tricks on pompous prelates and bullying barons. The anarchic individualism that was a feature of the first ballads about him might have been lost had such tales not been preserved in the Percy Folio – an ancient manuscript that Thomas Percy, Bishop of Dromore, claimed to have rescued, in the eighteenth century, from the hands of a housemaid who was about to use it to light the fire. The folio provided the basis for Percy's influential *Reliques of Ancient English Poetry* (1765). As well as legends of Arthur, it contains eight ballads about Robin Hood, dating from the fifteenth and sixteenth centuries. After reading poems based on these John Keats (1795–1821) was moved to write his own poem. In 'Robin Hood', he mourns the contrast between modern times and the old days when 'men knew nor rent nor leases'.

Gone, the merry morris din;
Gone, the song of Gamelyn;
Gone, the tough-belted outlaw
Idling in the 'grene shawe';
All are gone away and past!
And if Robin should be cast
Sudden from his turfed grave,
And if Marian should have

Once again her forest days,
She would weep, and he would craze:
He would swear, for all his oaks,
Fall'n beneath the dockyard strokes,
Have rotted on the briny seas;
She would weep that her wild bees
Sang not to her – strange! that honey
Can't be got without hard money!

LEFT
The popularity of the Robin Hood legend has endured to the present day, with new illustrated editions still published on a regular basis. This illustration by Walter Crane from 1915 shows Robin Hood fighting with his enemy, Guy of Gisborne, who hunts Robin Hood for the Sheriff of Nottingham.

OPPOSITE
The first page of Book III of the only surviving manuscript of Thomas Malory's 'Whole Book of King Arthur and his Noble Knights of the Round Table', which he completed in 1469. It was referred to by William Caxton for his 1485 printing of Malory's hugely popular retelling of the birth, life and death of Arthur.

In the begynnyng of Arthure

In the begynnyng of Arthure .ffir he was chosyn kynge
by aventure and by grace for the moste pty of the barowns kiewe nat he was
Ether pendragon son Butt as Merlyon made hitt opynly knowyn . Butt
yet many kyngis and lordis hylde hym grete werre for thatt cause . Butt well
Arthur ou com hem all the moste pty dayes of hys lyff he was ruled by y' counceile
of Merlyon So hit felle on a tyme kyng Arthur seyde unto Merlion my ba-
rownes woll let me have no reste butt nedis I muste take a wyff & I wolde none
take butt by thy counceile and advice . hit ys well done seyde Merlyon that
ye take a wyff . ffor a man of youre bounte and nobles scholde
nott be wt onte a wyff . Now is y' ony seyde Merlyon that
ye love more than a noy ye seyde kyng Arthure I love Gwe
nyvere the kyngs donghtir of lodegrean off y' londe off Came
lerde the whyche holdyth in his house the table rounde that ye
tolde me he had hit of my fadir Uther And this damesell is the
moste valyaunte and fayryst that I know lybyng or yet that ev'
I conde fynde Sertis seyde Merlyon as off her beaute and fayre
nesse she is one of the fayrest on lyve . But and ye loved her not
so well as ye do I scholde fynde you a damesell of beaute and
of goodnesse that scholde lyke you and please you and youre
herte were nat sette . Butt there as mannes herte is sette
he woll be loth to returne . that is trouthe seyde kyng Arthur
& Merlyon warned the kyng covertly that Gwenyver was nat
holsom for hym to take to wyff . ffor he warned hym that Laun-
celot scholde love her and she hym a gayne . and so he turned his
tale to the aventures off the Sankegreal . Than ij desyred of
the kyng for to have men wt hym y' scholde enquere of Gwenyv'
and so the kyng grunted hym and so Merlyon wente forthe
unto kyng lodegean off Camylerde and tolde hym of the desire
of the kyng y' he wolde have unto his wyff Gwenyv' his douzt'
That is to me seyde kyng lodegreans the beste tydyngs that
ev' I herde . that so worthy a kyng off probesse & noblesse wol wedde
my douzt' . And as for my londis I wolde geff hit hym yf I wyste

OPPOSITE
The Arthurian legend
of Sir Gawain and
the Green Knight has
fascinated audiences
for centuries. The
image shown in
this fourteenth-
century manuscript
is the oldest literary
representation of the
Green Knight, who is,
like the Green Man, a
symbol of nature.

Keats' reference to 'the merry morris din' is a reminder that Robin Hood has links with the pagan rites that have surrounded May Day festivities since time immemorial. Robin Hood still flaunts his subversive side as a Lord of Misrule in such centres of May Day celebrations as Lewes, Padstow and Whitstable. Nottinghamshire has made much of its most famous son, and an ancient oak near Edwinstowe in Sherwood Forest is imagined to be his hideout.

In her latest collection, *The Bees*, poet laureate Carol Ann Duffy (b.1955) celebrates John Barleycorn, 'green man, newly born ... ancient ... beer borne, good health, long life, John Barleycorn' in a litany of pub names redolent with half-remembered but still obscurely celebrated traditions.

> Britain's soul, as the crow flies, so flew he.
> I saw him in the Hollybush, the Yew Tree,
> The Royal Oak, the Ivy Bush, the Linden.
> I saw him in the Forester, the Woodman.

Another resilient myth of the greenwood is that of Sir Gawain and the Green Knight. The story goes that Arthur and his knights are celebrating Christmas at Camelot when a giant knight, his flesh, dress, horse and trappings all green, rides into court and offers a challenge which is taken up by Sir Gawain. A boisterous tale of sword-swipes and hunting prowess, chivalry and loyalty, magic and seduction, courage and cowardice, it has been interpreted as symbolising the confrontation between English chivalric tradition and Celtic mysticism. The earliest surviving version dates from a late-fourteenth-century manuscript, and the work was only printed in its entirety in 1839. Since then it has seized the imagination of its hearers to such an extent that it is being retold even today, when it is interpreted as a plea against despoiling nature for reasons of avarice and gain. Both J.R.R. Tolkien and Simon Armitage have written modern versions of it, and in 1991 the composer Sir Harrison Birtwistle adapted it into an opera.

Alan Garner (b.1934) writes fantasy tales for teenagers closely connected to the geology, archaeology and myths of his personal heartland, the Welsh border landscape of Cheshire's Alderley Edge. In his fiction, wrote Neil Gaiman in a fiftieth-anniversary edition of *The Weirdstone of Brisingamen*, one of Garner's best-known novels, 'real English places emerged from the shadows of folklore, and people found themselves waking, living and battling their way through the dreams and patterns of myth'. Garner's intense and claustrophobic novel *The Owl Service* (1967) retells the myth of the *Mabinogion* story of Blodeuwedd. A woman made of flowers by a Welsh wizard, she betrays her husband and is turned into an owl as a punishment for inciting her lover to kill him. Blodeuwedd's motives lie deep in the past, and her story is condemned to be repeated until the cycle is broken. Inspired by a stay in a medieval hallhouse in a remote Welsh valley, Garner's version of the myth is played

17

out by modern teenagers. They find a dinner service patterned with owls or flowers in the attic and a copy of the *Mabinogion* that seems possessed by spirits. Links with the legend of the Fisher King emerge. 'Look at this sick valley, Gwyn', says Alison. 'Tumbledown buildings, rough land. I saw two dead sheep on the way up the track. Maybe once the power's loose things'll be better, until the next time.'

Garner's books radically change the way in which his readers respond to landscapes. 'I read the book at the age of ten', writes a contributor to an *Owl Service* website. 'I grew up in the Weald of Kent, surrounded by orchards ripe for scrumping, and never felt threatened by the landscape. That all changed with *The Owl Service*. The once pleasant forest became haunted by woodsprites and malevolent mists'.

Rudyard Kipling's *Puck of Pook's Hill* (1906) is a much less menacing mix of myth and modern. Set on Kipling's own Sussex estate of Batemans near Burwash, it is the story of how Una and Dan accidentally summon Puck by acting out *A Midsummer Night's Dream* on Midsummer Eve. In a series of archaeological adventures, he leads the children through 'Merlin's Isle of Gramarye', bringing alive British history from the times of the Celts, Romans, Saxons, Vikings, Normans, medieval knights and eighteenth-century poachers. It is an intensely local book, exactly describing the ancient trackways of the Sussex Weald, the hummocks of its camps, its flint quarries and salt marshes. 'The People of the Hills have all left', says Puck. 'I saw them come into Old England and I saw them go. Giants, trolls, kelpies, brownies, goblins, imps; wood, tree, mound, and water spirits; heath-people, hill-watchers, treasure-guards, good people, little people, pishogues, leprechauns, night-riders, pixies, nixies, gnomes, and the rest – gone, all gone! I came into England with Oak, Ash and Thorn, and when Oak, Ash and Thorn are gone, I shall go too.'

John Cowper Powys (1872–1963) made the vast Dorset earthwork of Maiden Castle the setting of a modern romance in which the lovers are haunted by the pagan past. Powys was obsessed by the ancient significance of the landscape in which he lived, and he walked and explored it assiduously. In a typically overblown image he likens Dorchester and its many-layered history to 'one deep vase of thick-pressed pot-pourri'. The Ordnance Survey had completed their mapping of Britain by the time he wrote, and when, in *Maiden Castle*, his hero Dud No-Man enters the house of his friend Mrs Dearth, he sees 'an enormous map of the county of Dorset, printed in Dorchester in the early days of Queen Victoria'. Powys used his knowledge of the then very recent Dorset findings of the archaeologist Sir Mortimer Wheeler in the scene in which Uryen looks at a Celtic votive image. Unearthed along with a Roman figure of Minerva, it 'had been under the chalk when Caesar landed, under the chalk when the Conqueror landed, under the chalk when Victoria was crowned'. Powys's last and most arcane work *Porius: A Romance of the Dark Ages* is set on the slopes of Snowdon, and brings on Merlin, King Arthur, the bard Taliesin, aboriginal giants and Three Aunties – silver-haired Fates – as druids, priests of Mithras and Christians do battle.

LEFT
Puck appears to
Una and Dan on
Midsummer's Eve.
Illustration by H. Millar
for Rudyard Kipling's
Puck of Pook's Hill
(1906), a book that
brought mythical and
real English history
alive for children in a
series of adventures
set in the Sussex hills.

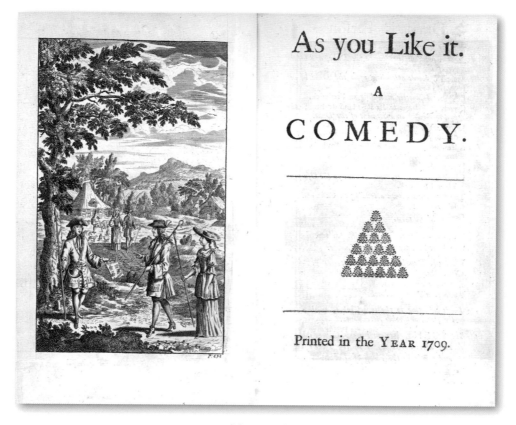

Earthly Paradise

Renaissance Englishmen emulated Roman poets when they composed pastorals contrasting honest rural simplicities with the corruption of city life. Alexander Barclay (1476–1552), a well-educated and much-travelled cleric, had close links to the court but retained a yearning for country life. He became a monk in the Benedictine monastery of Ely, where he revised his *Eclogues* (1514). The fifth of his dialogues, 'The Cytezen and Uplondyshman', features the warnings of a shepherd who moved to the city then back to the country again, as he tells an old comrade about the city's dangers.

> There men be choked with vile and deadly scent
> Here have we odour of flowers redolent.
> I count me happy which when in the village,
> Is undefiled with citizens' outrage.

In *As You Like It* (1600), William Shakespeare (1564–1616) used the Forest of Arden, the woods in which he himself had roamed (and notoriously poached) as a boy, as a foil to the corruption of the court. 'Are not these woods/More free from peril than the envious court?' asks Duke Senior. 'Here feel we but the penalty of Adam/The seasons' difference … Even till I shrink with cold, I smile and say, "This is no flattery".' In the greenwood, the Duke finds 'tongues in trees, books in running brooks, Sermons in stones, and good in everything'. *As You Like It* was performed in 1603 at Wilton House, near Salisbury, an appropriate setting to be identified with Arcadian bliss. It was the seat of Henry Herbert, Earl of Pembroke, who had married Sir Philip Sidney's brilliant sister Mary. Sidney's tribute to Wilton, the heroic romance *The Countess of Pembroke's Arcadia*, likened the great estate to the bucolic, deeply feudal community into which his hero Duke Basileus retreats to escape the cares of the world.

Ben Jonson (1572–1637) came from Annandale in Dumfries and Galloway, but spent most of his life in London. Best known for satirical and often lewd city entertainments, he praised country life in a Horatian ode celebrating the home of his patron Robert Sidney (brother of Mary and Philip). *To Penshurst* salutes the close connection of that 'ancient pile' with the rural traditions that surrounded it, 'joying' in fine 'soil, air, wood and water, walks for health, as well as sport', and a mount

> …to which thy Dryads do resort,
> Where Pan and Bacchus their high feasts have made,
> Beneath the broad beech, and the chestnut shade.

The Yorkshire-born metaphysical poet Andrew Marvell (1621–78) wrote a similar poem in praise of the Cromwellian general Thomas Fairfax's retirement to Appleton, near Selby, likened by Marvell to Romulus' 'bee-like cell'. Comparing Appleton favourably with such pretentious show houses as Hardwick Hall, Marvell describes the mowers busy in its pastures and the teeming fish in its river.

> Nature here hath been so free
> As if she said leave this to me.
> Art would more neatly have defac'd
> What she had laid so sweetly wast;
> In fragrant Gardens, Shady Woods,
> Deep Meadows, and transparent Floods.

Apostrophising Fairfax's heir, his only daughter Maria, Marvell concludes that she will take on the estate's commitment to its dependants much more genuinely than did the nuns ('Hypocrite Witches') who once lived there.

London-born Katherine Fowler (1632–64) married the Welsh Parliamentarian James Philips in 1647 and proceeded to establish a Society of Friends in The Priory, their country house near Cardigan in Wales. Dedicated to ideals of Platonic love, its members adopted names from pastoral poems, with Katherine becoming known as 'the

Matchless Orinda', intelligent, virtuous and chaste. Her poem 'A Country Life' likens rural existence to that of dwellers in the Golden Age, when 'Nature was all their wit'. While the fashionable rush to Hyde Park, she is content to stay in her 'hermitage'.

> In this retir'd and humble seat,
> Free from both war and strife
> I am not forc'd to make retreat,
> But choose to spend my life.

A variation on pastorals praising rural life was the description of its seasons, most famously by James Thomson (1700–48). The Scottish poet and playwright drew on memories of his youth in the Borders, wildly romanticising rural labours.

> Now swarms the village o'er the jovial mead;
> The rustic youth, brown with meridian toil,
> Healthful and strong; full as the summer-rose
> Blown by prevailing suns, the ruddy maid,
> Half-naked, swelling on the sight, and all
> Her kindled graces burning o'er her cheek.
> Even stooping age is here; and infant-hands
> Trail the long rake ...

The reclusive poet A.E. Housman (1859–1936) transformed our appreciation of the countryside around Ludlow in Shropshire, imaginatively mapping such places as Wenlock Edge and the Wrekin ('On Wenlock Edge the wood's in trouble./His forest fleece the Wrekin heaves'), Bredon Hill ('In summer time on Bredon,/The bells they sounds so clear'), and 'Clunton and Clunbury,/Clungenford and Clun,/Are the quietest places/Under the Sun'. These were the 'blue remembered hills' of his childhood, only briefly revisited in later life, but evidently never forgotten. Housman is probably best known for his poem *A Shropshire Lad* (1896), written in memory both of the death of the brother of his beloved friend Moses Jackson and the many 'Ludlow Lads' who lost their lives fighting for Queen Victoria in her Imperial wars. Housman was then Professor of Latin at University College London; he later held the Kennedy Professorship of Latin at Cambridge.

Housman's slim volumes were tucked in many a khaki pocket during the First World War, among them that of Edward Thomas (1878–1917). Thomas wrote topographical descriptions of England (*The Icknield Way, The South Country, Wales*) before turning to poetry himself on the urging of Robert Frost. When his train paused one day in June 1914 at the tiny Gloucestershire halt of Adlestrop, he was inspired to write a poem that immortalised the place at one moment in time.

OPPOSITE
In his 1896 collection of poems, *A Shropshire Lad*, A.E. Housman imaginatively mapped the 'blue remembered hills' of his childhood. Illustration to the 1940 edition by Agnes Miller Parker.

22

... What I saw was Adlestrop – only the name
And willows, willow-herb, and grass,
And meadowsweet, and haycocks dry,
No white less still and lonely fair
Than the high cloudlets in the sky.

And for that minute a blackbird sang
Close by, and round him, mistier,
Farther and farther, all the birds
Of Oxfordshire and Gloucestershire.

Oscar Wilde (1854–1900) amusingly satirised the myth of the rural idyll in his comedy *The Importance of Being Earnest* (1895). The urbane man-about-town Ernest Worthing assumes a completely different persona in the country, where he pretends he is Ernest's brother, the upright (and tediously earnest) John Worthing, of Woolton Manor, in Hertfordshire. This is for the benefit of his young ward Cecily, whom he is trying to protect from the corruption of smart London life. There is no lauding of rural life. Cecily, finding it distinctly dull, longs to meet the family's black sheep, her dashing uncle Ernest, while Gwendolen, whom Ernest is courting, tells Cecily that the country bores her to death. 'Ah! This is what the newspapers call agricultural depression, is it not?' says Cecily. 'I believe the aristocracy are suffering very much from it just at present. It is almost an epidemic among them.'

The dream survived such mockery, but in its twentieth-century form it was tempered by greater realism. Flora Thompson (1876–1947), the daughter of a stonemason and a nursemaid, lived on the borders of Oxfordshire and Northamptonshire in a hamlet called Juniper Hill ('Lark Rise'), ten miles from Buckingham ('Candleford'). Her three semi-autobiographical books describe the childhood and adolescence of 'Laura', detailing with exquisite accuracy and wit both everyday life in the little rural community and the gradual invasion of change there. They were also a tribute to her favourite brother Edwin ('Edmund'), who died in the Battle of the Somme. Harvest was especially memorable as a time when the whole community pulled together.

YOUR COUNTRY'S CALL

Isn't this worth fighting for?
ENLIST NOW

24

LEFT
World War One recruitment poster showing the idealised countryside conjured up by Edward Thomas in his poem 'Adlestrop', 1915.

'For three weeks or more, the hamlet was astir before dawn and the homely odours of bacon frying, wood fires and tobacco smoke overpowered the pure, damp, earthy scent of the fields. It would be school holidays then, and the children at the end house always wanted to get up hours before their time. Awed, yet uplifted by the silence and clean-washed loveliness of the dawn, the children would pass along the narrow field paths with rustling wheat on each side. Or Laura would make little dashes into the corn for poppies, or pull trails of the lesser bindweed, with its pink-striped trumpets, like clean cotton frocks, to trim her hat and girdle her waist, while Edmund would stump on, red-faced with indignation at her carelessness in making trails in the standing corn.'

I was set down from the carrier's cart at the age of three; and then with a first sense of bewilderness & desertion, my life in the village began.

The June grass, among which I stood, was taller than I was, and I wept. I had never been so near to grass before. It towered above me, and all around me, and each sharp blade was tattooed with tiger stripes of sunlight. It was dark & a wicked green, thick as a forest, and ~~it was~~ alive with grasshoppers that chirped & chattered & leapt through the air like monkeys.

I was lost and did not know which way to move. A burning heat oozed up from the ground, rank with sharp odours of roots & nettles. Snow clouds of elder ~~blossom~~ & wild parsley hung banked in the sky, showering upon me the fumes & flakes of their giddy suffocating blooms. High overhead ~~the~~ larks sang, with a frenzy as if the sky was tearing apart.

For the first time in my life I was out of sight of humans. For the first time in my life I was alone in a world whose behaviour I could neither predict nor fathom; a world of birds that squealed, of plants that stank, of insects that sprang about like arrows. I was lost and I did not expect to be found again. I put back my

Laurie Lee (1914–97) wrote his equally lyrical, unsentimental and frequently comic memoir of growing up, *Cider with Rosie*, in 1959. The novel spoke powerfully to an age when the majority of people now lived in towns, cities and suburbs, and influences such as cinema, television and motor cars were invading village life. Lee's description of growing up with his mother and seven brothers and sisters in a seventeenth-century stone cottage in a steep-sided valley in the depths of Gloucestershire is both lyrical and pragmatic. It begins with three-year-old Laurie feeling dwarfed by the June grass. 'It towered above me and all around me, each blade tattooed with tiger-skins of sunlight'. Its most famous passage describes the adolescent Laurie embracing his cousin Rosie under a hay wagon. 'Never to be forgotten, that first long secret drink of golden fire, juice of those valleys and of that time, wine of wild orchards, of russet summer, of lump and red apples, and Rosie's burning cheeks.' The memoir ends with the foreshadowing of change, the dropping away of the 'white-whiskered, gaitered, booted and bonneted, ancient-tongued last of their world', and the appearance of the revving motorbikes of his sisters' suitors. 'We began to shrug off the valley and look more to the world, where pleasures were more anonymous and tasty. They were coming fast, and we were ready for them.'

Living off the Land

As well as romanticising the countryside, writers acknowledged its muddy realities. Edmund Spenser's *Shepheardes Calender* (1579) recreated the lives of medieval field-workers, adopting archaic spellings derived from Geoffrey Chaucer, saluting William Langland with a character called Piers and giving a nod to the fifteenth-century poet John Skelton by borrowing his folk character Colin Clout. Spenser makes Clout a shepherd, and describes his life through the year. However, he was more interested in parodying a whole range of literary models and delivering satirical jibes at his contemporaries than in accurately portraying the rural scene.

A much keener eye is cast upon agriculture by the instructive rhyming couplets of *A Hundred Points of Good Husbandry* (1557). The poet farmer Thomas Tusser (1524–80) was educated at Eton and Cambridge; after ten years at court he settled as a farmer at Cattawade, Suffolk. The poem is wonderfully specific, and many of its adages ('Safe bind, safe find', 'Christmas comes but once a year', 'Tis an ill wind that blows no good') have become proverbial. A local note is struck in the couplets for August. After advising on spreading muck-hills to improve the yield of barley fields, Tusser refers to a Suffolk speciality, the saffron plot, a twenty-foot square of which yielded a sufficient crop for 'both thine house, and next neighbour too'.

Robert Blomfield (1766–1823) was a self-taught 'peasant poet' from Honington, near Thetford. His poem *The Farmer's Boy* (1800), published with woodcuts by Thomas Bewick, was set in the grounds of Euston Hall, the Suffolk seat of his patron, the Earl of Grafton. Although influenced by Thomson's *The Seasons*, Blomfield was far

OPPOSITE
'I was set down from the carrier's cart ...' The first page of the manuscript of Laurie Lee's *Cider with Rosie* (1959), his lyrical and frequently comic memoir of growing up in deepest Gloucestershire.

Iulia, themperor Augustus his daughter, and vvyfe to Agryppa. So doth Arun-
tius Stella euery where call his Lady Asteris and Ianthis, albe it is vvel knowen
that her right name vvas Violantilla: as vvitnesseth Statius in his Epithalamiū,
And so the famous Paragone of Italy, Madonna Cœlia in her letters enclo-
peth her selfe vnder the name of Zima: and Petrona vnder the name of Bello-
chia. And this generally hath bene a common custome of counterfeicting the
names of secret Personages.

Auail) bring downe. ᵒ

Emblema:

Ouerhaile) drawe ouer.

His Embleme or Poesye is here vnder added in Italian, *Anchóra speme:* the meaning
vvherof is, that notvvithstande his extreme passion and lucklesse loue, yet lea-
ning on hope, he is some what recomforted.

Februarie.

Ægloga Secunda.

ARGVMENT.

THis Æglogue is rather morall and generall, then bent to any secrete or
particular purpose. It specially conteyneth a discourse of old age, in the
persone of Thenot an olde Shepheard, who for his crookednesse and vnlusti-
nesse, is scorned of Cuddie an vnhappy Heardmans boye. The matter very well accordeth with the season of the moneth, the yeare now drouping, &
as it were, drawing to his last age. For as in this time of yeare, so the in our

more realistic about the arduous nature of such tasks as prising frozen turnips from the ground to feed stock in winter.

Thomas Hardy (1840–1928) was born in a tiny cottage in Higher Bockhampton just east of Dorchester, today a museum. Both his novels and poems show his deep knowledge about, and love of, the Dorset countryside and its ways of life. 'I am convinced', he once wrote, 'that it is better for a writer to know a little bit of the world remarkably well than to know a great part of the world remarkably little'. *Far from the Madding Crowd* (1874), his first literary success, offers in ample measure details of the English rural world that Hardy cherished. He took his title from Thomas Gray's *Elegy Written in a Country Churchyard* (1751):

> Far from the madding crowd's ignoble strife
> Their sober wishes never learn'd to stray;
> Along the cool sequester'd vale of life
> They kept the noiseless tenor of their way.

'Madding' means 'frenzied' here, and in one sense the title may be ironic: the novel's main characters – honest Oak, tempestuous Bathsheba, dashing Sergeant Troy, smouldering Boldwood and the desperate Fanny Robin – are all passionate beings who find the vale of life neither quiet nor cool. But there is no mistaking Hardy's deepest purpose: a celebration of traditional ways of farming the land. He christened

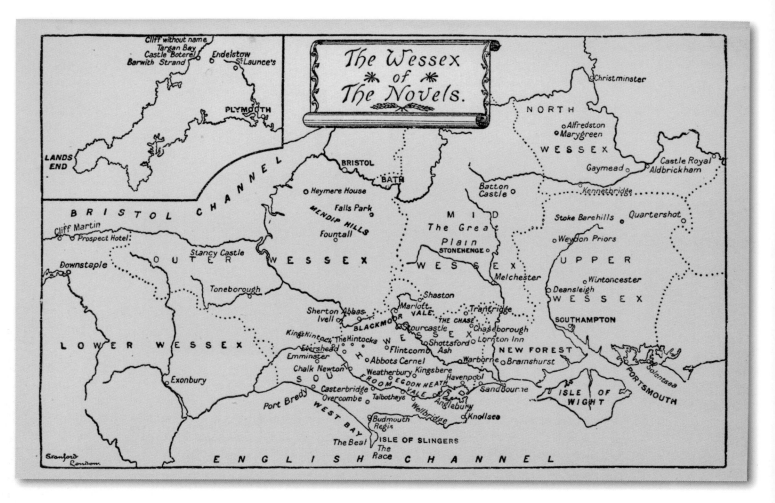

The Wessex of The Novels.

ABOVE
Map from a 1925 edition of *Under the Greenwood Tree*. Thomas Hardy only gradually developed his 'partly real, partly dream-country' of Wessex. He first drew a map of it for the endpapers of the 1895 collected edition of the Wessex novels.

the 'partly real, partly dream-country' in which he set the book 'Wessex' in order to emphasise its connections with England's distant past. Country customs such as divination by Bible and key, sheep-washing, shearing-suppers, harvest homes and market-days drive the story, and in his preface to the 1895 edition of the book Hardy laments that the change from settled cottagers to migratory agricultural labourers 'has led to a break in continuity in local history, more fatal than any other thing to the preservation of legend, folk-lore, close inter-social relations, and eccentric individualities'.

'No one English writer before had such a wide knowledge of labourers, farmers, gamekeepers, poachers, of the fields, and woods, and waters, and the sky above them, by day and night' wrote Edward Thomas of Richard Jefferies (1848–87). Descended from generations of Wiltshire farmers who lived near the hamlet of Coate, near Swindon, Wiltshire, Jefferies became acclaimed for such accurate and informative but intensely poetic books about country life as *The Gamekeeper at Home* and *The Amateur*

Poacher. Jefferies is most enduringly famous for his children's book *Bevis: The Story of a Boy* (1882). In it he recreated his own childhood escapades in and around the great reservoir of Coate Water. The endpaper map of *Bevis* closely resembles the shape of Coate Water, though Coate's rather meagre islands are imaginatively inflated into New Formosa and Serendip.

The rural idyll of Bevis was an important influence on Arthur Ransome (1884–1967), who borrowed Jefferies' idea of children turning a real landscape into one haunted by savages, sailors and explorers for his own *Swallows and Amazons* (1930), which he set in an imaginary 'Lake in the North' made up of the lake and islands of Windermere (where he then lived) and the mountains, moors and streams around Coniston (where he had spent his childhood). Ransome wrote the book as a reaffirmation of the importance of rural life after the upheavals of the First World War and a celebration of his own return after eleven years as a journalist in Russia and Eastern Europe. He set four sequels to the story in the Lake District and four others on East Anglian waters. All his books are painstakingly accurate in their

BELOW
Richard Jefferies
came from a farming
family; his upbringing
in the Wiltshire
countryside inspired
the imaginative
escapades in *Bevis:
The Story of a Boy*.
Cover of the 1908
edition.

representation of traditional ways, be it charcoal burning in the woods around Coniston Water or 'babbing' for eels on the Norfolk Broads. His books changed the way in which generations of children have seen the Lake District and Broadland landscapes. To this day, Ransome fans from all over the world sail on Coniston and Windermere to islands strikingly similar to Wild Cat Island, climb the surrounding hills in search of the secret valley of *Swallowdale* (1931), and follow his routes to the rivers of Norfolk and Suffolk.

Mary Webb (1881–1927), a near contemporary of Arthur Ransome, wrote novels of country life that were as deeply felt and passionately observed as those of Thomas Hardy, who admired her work, as did John Buchan, G.K. Chesterton and J.M. Barrie. Born and brought up by loving and cultured parents close to the Wrekin, in the heart of Shropshire, Webb was aware of the threat that the heavy industry of Coalbrookdale and the Black Country presented to country ways. The unnaturalness of supposedly civilised life was as much her theme as Hardy's, but, as the opening lines of *Gone to Earth* (1917) show, she went further than he did in romancing local stones.

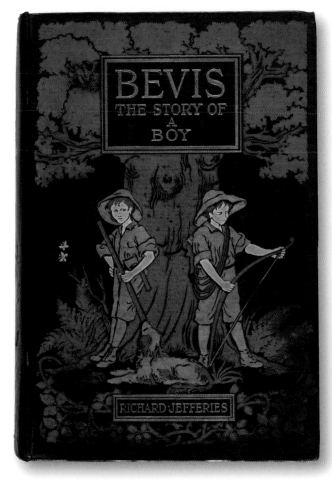

31

32

ABOVE
In 1917, Mary Webb's
Gone to Earth was
voted Novel of the
Year by Rebecca West;
it was republished in
1930 with dramatic
(if a shade stolid)
illustrations by
Norman Hepple and
an introduction by
John Buchan.

'Small feckless clouds were hurried across the vast untroubled sky – shepherdless, futile, imponderable – and were torn to fragments on the fangs of the mountains, so ending their ephemeral adventures with nothing of their fugitive existence left but a few tears.'

At the book's climax, Hazel Woodus, the elemental, gypsyish heroine, leaps into a quarry clutching her pet fox, a symbol of wild nature, that she is trying to save from the local hunt. 'Mary Webb is a genius', wrote Rebecca West in the *Times Literary Supplement* in 1917, and voted the book Novel of the Year. 'No-one of our day has a greater power of evoking natural magic', wrote John Buchan. 'The landscape, the weather, the seasons, are made to crowd in upon us as we follow the doings of the protagonists, and we are perpetually aware of these things as a fateful background.'

Mary Webb's books became hugely popular, but her passionate descriptions and dramatic accounts of rural seductions lent themselves dangerously easily to parody. In 1928 Stella Gibbons, a journalist on the *Evening Standard*, was given the task of summarising the plot of Webb's first novel, *The Golden Arrow* (1916), as a preface to instalments of its serial publication in the paper. The job inspired her to write *Cold Comfort Farm* (1932), her hilarious pastiche of such books as *Gone to Earth* and Sheila Kaye-Smith's similarly intense *Sussex Gorse* (1916). The novel is set in a 'near future' in which Mayfair has become a slum, Lambeth is fashionable and smart people spin about in light aircraft. Armed with her trusty handbook *The Higher Common Sense*, Flora Poste acts as a *dea ex machina* when she arrives at the Starkadders' crumbling and ancient Sussex farm, transforming the lives of its eccentric occupants. Hell-fire preacher Amos is sent off in one of the new Ford vans to spread the Word of the Lord, so that the farm can be run efficiently by his frustrated oldest son Reuben. His brother, the handsome, randy Seth, is introduced to a Hollywood film director with immediate success, and their young sister, the fey, nature-worshipping Elfine, is given a crash course in social graces and dress sense which brings her neighbour Richard Hawk-Monitor of Hautecouture Hall to his knees, proffering a ring. In a splendid finale, the miserly and manipulative Aunt Ada Doom, the family matriarch who once saw something nasty in the woodshed and had been fed on dainties and kowtowed to ever since, exits in a biplane to taste the high life in Paris.

Winifred Holtby (1898–1935) was the daughter of a prosperous Yorkshire farmer. Her acclaimed novel *South Riding* (1936) is a moving portrait of a Yorkshire community

OPPOSITE
The last page of the
original manuscript
of Stella Gibbons'
Cold Comfort Farm
(1932), her comic
parody of Mary Webb's
overblown style.
Only the first and
the last pages of the
manuscript survive.

2

lips move, and guessed what he was saying×

as the farm chopped away beneath them. He
full
was occupied with keeping the machine clear of the topmost branches of the elms, and
dropped one hand on hers. He could not
look at her,
take his eyes from the steering, but she saw

by his troubled profile that he feared (so

fantastically beautiful was their the night and
this
their discovery of their love) that it might be

some cruel mistake.
[Flora put her warm lips close to his cap.
her
" I love you " she said. He could not hear a
very well he
comforted,
dead, but turned for a second and, smiled
×
into her eyes.
[She glanced upwards for a second at the soft
blue
summer vault of the Midsummer Night sky. Not
misted depths.
Not Nor a cloud broke its solemn beauty. Tomorrow

would be a beautiful day.
        THE END

struggling to cope with the effects of the agricultural depression of the 1930s. She derived its plot, a story of local government skulduggery, from minutes of council meetings discarded by her mother, an East Riding alderman. *South Riding* is a fictional invention, but Kingsport is instantly recognisable as Hull, and Cold Harbour colony, the ex-servicemen's colony of smallholdings, is based on Sunk Island, a part of Holderness. Holtby died of tuberculosis aged only thirty-seven, and it was her executor and close friend Vera Brittain who made sure that the novel was published. Several of the characters were too true to life for the comfort of Holtby's mother, who was incensed by the book's publication and immediately resigned from the council. The book's descriptions of the East Yorkshire landscape are unforgettable.

> Acre beyond acre from her bedroom window, Midge could see the broad swelling sea of rain-rinsed green, the wet, bluish grass of wheat in blade, the dry tawny green of unploughed stubble, the ruffled billowing green of uncut meadow grasses, the dark clumps of trees, elm and ash and sycamore. There was not a hill, not a church, not a village. From Maythorpe southward to Lincolnshire lay only fields and dykes and scattered farms and the unseen barrier of the Leame Estuary, the plain rising and dimpling in gentle undulations as though a giant potter had pressed his thumb now more lightly, now more heavily, on the yet malleable clay of the spinning adobe.

Adrian Bell's *Men and the Fields* (1939) was published on the eve of the twentieth century's second great war. For some time authors and artists had been involved in a widespread movement to record the best of Britain for posterity – in posters and paintings, photographs and etchings, as well as exact descriptions by talented writers. Adrian Bell had written three novels (*Corduroy, Silver Ley, The Cherry Tree*) about his apprenticeship and coming of age as a farmer before he joined forces with his friend and neighbour the artist John Nash to produce a collage of their experiences as farmers at Creems and Bottengom's Farm, on the Stour, during the Depression years of the 1930s. Ronald Blythe, whose own work *Akenfield* (1969) recorded memories of similar times in a Suffolk village, called *Men and the Fields* 'an unconscious threnody to a scene which was to disappear for ever'. The Second World War would bring agricultural subsidies and a prosperous recovery for farmers; gradually machines would rule. The pace of farming life would alter dramatically, something Bell deeply regretted.

> A small elderly man in shirtsleeves on a roan cob stops on his way from one harvest field to another. A glass tankard is brought out. The roan cob is discussed ... There is no hurry; the sun is blinding on the white gables, the cob stands, the tankard is raised. Chat and drink, the sharp house-shadow creeping to the horse's feet. A core of old England yet, in all this.

OPPOSITE
Illustration by John Nash for *Men and the Fields* (1939), a book about traditional Suffolk farming ways written by his friend and neighbour the writer and farmer Adrian Bell.

Strokes of Havoc

Criticism of man's destructive impact on his environment began early. In *Piers Plowman*, William Langland (c.1330–86) deplores the enclosure of common land by the gentry, so that poor people had nowhere to graze their animals. Protest soon developed into a vigorous oral and broadsheet literature of diatribes against the oppression of poor countrymen by the wealthy. *Jack of the North* (1549), a dialogue published shortly before Kett's Rebellion, attacked the impact of enclosures in Cambridgeshire. The Elizabethan morality play *A Merry Knack to Know a Knave* (1594) featured Piers Plowman complaining to the king about unjust landlords; when it was first performed in London in June 1592 a riot broke out and the City Council ordered all theatres to be closed.

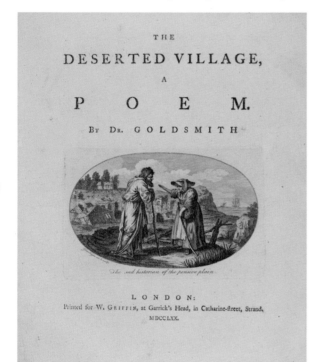

ABOVE
Title-page of the 1770 edition of *The Deserted Village*, Oliver Goldsmith's famous attack on the destructive effect of emparkment on rural communities.

The most magnificent seventeenth-century ecological lament was the encyclopaedic *Sylva: Or a Discourse on Forest Trees*. Its author, the diarist John Evelyn (1620–1706), warned that the dockyards were making unsustainable demands on British woodlands, and urged all landowners to become planters, so that the navy's needs could be provided for without laying waste the countryside. Evelyn was a founder member of the Royal Society, an institution dedicated to solving social and economic problems with the aid of science. *Sylva*, the first book to be published under the society's auspices, described both native British trees and exotics. It featured such remarkably ancient trees as the Cawthorpe Oak, 'compared to which all other trees are children of the Forest', and offered advice on planting both forests for timber and sacred groves for recreation. Still extant, the Cawthorpe Oak is now 18 metres in circumference.

Oliver Goldsmith's *The Deserted Village* (1770), thought to have been based on the demolition of Nuneham Courtenay village in 1756, uses vivid details to drive home his polemic against enclosures. In it he contrasts the importance of the village school and its stern but kind master, and the tavern 'where nut-brown draughts inspired', with the economically useless new park enclosed by 'the man of wealth and pride' from 'space that many poor supplied'.

Concern over the speed of rural change was what led the London literati's enthusiasm for the Northamptonshire 'peasant poet' John Clare (1793–1864). His exquisitely observant, snail's pace poems eulogised 'the religion of the fields' and deplored the encroachment of enclosures on the commons. In 'Summer Morning', the freshness of dawn is detailed with a miniaturist's eye and a poet's ear.

O'er pathless plains at early hours
The sleepy rustic sloomy [sic] goes;
The dews, brushed off from grass and flowers,
Be moistening sop his hardened shoes
While every leaf that forms a shade,
And every floweret's silken top,
And every shivering bent and blade,
Stoops, bowing with a diamond drop.

By contrast, 'Remembrance' mourns the devastation of the old rural balance by the new farming methods.

By Langley Bush I roam, but the bush hath left its hill,
On Cowper Green I stray, 'tis a desert strange and chill,
And the spreading Lea Close oak, ere decay had penned its will,
To the axe of the spoiler and self-interest fell a prey,
And Crossberry Way and old Round Oak's narrow lane
With its hollow trees like pulpits I shall never see again,
Enclosure like a Buonaparte let not a thing remain,
It levelled every bush and tree and levelled every hill
And hung the moles for traitors – though the brook is running still
It runs a sicker brook, cold and chill.

Thomas Hardy grew up in an age when the older generation still remembered the Napoleonic wars well, and he was appalled to see what hardships the rural poor endured in the face of mechanised agriculture. The tragic story of *Tess of the D'Urbervilles* (1891), in which the artless and innocent Tess is seduced by Alec D'Urberville, pointed up the rape of the rural environment as the riches of the countryside were whirled away by rail to meet the insatiable demand of the cities. Conversely the way in which Hardy brings the landscape to life intensifies the degradation that Tess undergoes. 'Each is landscape, plus a man's soul', observed Hardy of Turner's watercolours while he was writing *Tess*, and the description could be applied to his own scene-settings. The pretty Vale of Blackmoor reflects Tess's innocence, and the ancient trees of the Chase and its dying pheasants counterpoint her fall from grace. The prosperous farm Talbothays gives her a brief taste of Paradise, while the stony ground of Flintcomb-Ash is a place of exile where identity is crushed. 'A field-woman is a portion of the field; she has somehow lost her own margin, imbibed the essence of her surrounding, and assimilated herself within it'. Finally Tess is effectively sacrificed on the ancient altar at Stonehenge.

Gerard Manley Hopkins (1844–89) celebrated the natural world unforgettably

Of busy industry seeks the sweet
Of keep weary labour ought be gain
As oft the bliss the idle meets
& heaven bestows the bliss in vain

Pleas'd I list the rural themes
Hasting up the ploughmans toil
Urging on the jingling teams
As they turn the yellow soil

Industrys care abounds again
As now the peace of night is fled & gone
Many a murmur wakes the plain
Hardy a waggon rumbles on

The swallow wheels his curling flight
From oer the waters surface skims
Then on the cottage chimney lights
& twittering chaunts his morning hymns

Stationd high a towering height
On the sun gilt weather cock
Now the jackdaw takes his flight
Frighted by the chiming clock

Snug the way watching thrush
Sits to nurse her speckled breast
Where the woodbine round the bush
Weaving hides her mortard nest
Till the cows with hungry low
Picks the rank

in such poems as 'The Windhover' and 'God's Grandeur'. But he also mourned its destruction. His poem 'Spring and Fall: To a Young Child', begins in gentle wonder 'Margaret are you grieving/Over Goldengrove unleaving?', and ends in profound sadness, 'It is the fate that man was born for,/It is Margaret you mourn for'. Another of his works, 'Binsey Poplars', begins with a joyfully fanciful description of branches like 'airy cages' quenching 'in leaves the leaping sun', but ends with a lament.

> O if we but knew what we do
> When we delve or hew –
> Hack and rack the growing green!
> Since country is so tender
> To touch, her being só slender,
> That, like this sleek and seeing ball
> But a prick will make no eye at all,
> Where we, even where we mean
> To mend her we end her,
> When we hew or delve:
> After-comers cannot guess the beauty been.
> Ten or twelve, only ten or twelve
> Strokes of havoc únselve
> The sweet especial scene,
> Rural scene, a rural scene,
> Sweet especial rural scene.

Nostalgia for fast-disappearing country ways infuses E.M. Forster's novel *Howards End* (1910). Although the book is primarily a portrait of contemporary shifts in English class relationships, the dwellings of its characters are deeply symbolic. The bright and intellectual Schlegels have much in common with Ruth Wilcox, the old-gentry wife of the brashly physical *nouveau riche* Londoner Henry Wilcox, and when Mrs Wilcox dies she elects to leave her family house Howards End to Margaret Schlegel, knowing that Margaret will be much more sensitive to its rich history than Henry and her own arrogant children. Towards the end of the novel Margaret visits a nearby farm, and Forster described the world that was being lost through her eyes:

Here had lived an elder race, to which we look back with disquietude. The country which we visit at weekends was really a home to it, and the graver sides of life, the deaths, the partings, the yearnings for love, have their deepest expressions in the hearts of the fields. All was not sadness. The sun was shining without. The thrush sang his two syllables on the budding guelder-rose. Some children were playing uproariously in heaps of

OPPOSITE
John Clare often lamented the passing of old ways and rural peace. His 1821 poem 'Summer Morning' is an exquisitely unhurried description of dawn in the Northamptonshire meadows.

RIGHT
E.M. Forster lived
at Rooks Nest in
Hertfordshire, from the
age of four; a symbol
for him of unbroken
traditions, it closely
resembled the house
around which the plot
of his novel *Howards
End* (1910) revolves.

golden straw. It was the presence of sadness at all that surprised Margaret, and ended by giving her a feeling of completeness. In these English farms, if anywhere, one might see life steadily and see it whole, group in one vision its transitoriness and its eternal youth, connect – connect without bitterness until all men are brothers.

Howards End itself was modelled on Rooks Nest, E.M. Forster's boyhood home in Hertfordshire, once owned by a family called Howard. Forster lived in this small, unpretentious house from the age of four to fourteen. 'From the time I entered the house at the age of four ... I took it to my heart and hoped ... that I would live and die there', he said in a polemical 1946 radio broadcast, 'The Challenge of Our Times'. 'I still think [its setting] the loveliest in England ... hedges full of clematis, primroses and bluebells, dog roses and nuts.' There was nothing special about it, Forster maintained; in fact it was its sheer ordinariness that made it precious to him. In the broadcast he was attacking the proposal to build the London satellite town of Stevenage all around Rooks Nest. After conceding the need for new housing, he said, 'I cannot free myself from the conviction that something irreplaceable has been destroyed, and that a little piece of England has died as surely as if a bomb had hit it. I wonder what compensation there is in the world of the spirit for the destructiveness of the life here, the life of tradition.' Furniture from the Rooks Nest drawing-room – a many-shelved mantelpiece, fender, carpet and writing desk – followed him from house to house until they were installed in his rooms in King's College, Cambridge; I had tea with him among them in 1964.

The twentieth-century decline of the great estates once praised by writers of pastorals was caustically charted by Evelyn Waugh (1903–66). In his *Decline and Fall* (1928) Llanabba Castle has become a fifth-rate public school, and the beautiful Tudor manor of King's Thursday is going to be replaced by 'something clean and square', designed by the architect of a chewing-gum factory. The novel *Vile Bodies* (1930) features Doubting Hall, home of one of England's most notable Catholic families; it is pressed into use as a film set for a life of John Wesley, the founder of Methodism. In *A Handful of Dust* (1934) Hetton Abbey is a sham-Gothic pile in which Toby Last (names are significant in Waugh) lives the out-dated Victorian fantasy of chivalry *redux*; his wife Brenda, however, will betray him just as Guinevere betrayed Arthur. Waugh's *Brideshead Revisited* (1945) was more nostalgic, contrasting the glories of the house in its heyday, an ark of tradition in its own self-sufficient estate, with the chaos of the post-war years, when all the old certainties look as shattered as the jagged patterns in a kaleidoscope. In his preface to the revised edition of the book, published in the more hopeful time of 1959, Waugh explains that it was written in 'a bleak period of present privation and threatening disaster – the era of soya beans and Basic English – and in consequence the book is infused with a kind of gluttony, for food and wine, for the splendours of the recent past, and for the rhetorical and ornamental language which now, with a full stomach, I find distasteful'.

ABOVE
Madresfield Court in Malvern, Worcestershire, the ancestral home of the Lygon family, was frequently visited by Evelyn Waugh who met Hugh Lygon, a younger son of the Earl of Beauchamp, at Oxford. The house has been proposed as an inspiration for *Brideshead Revisited* (1945).

DARK SATANIC MILLS

The first changes that the industrial revolution made to Britain's landscape were seen by many contemporary writers as inspiring symbols of progress. Masson, the great mill that Richard Arkwright built to harness the power of the Derwent river in Derbyshire, was celebrated in Erasmus Darwin's *The Botanic Garden* (1791).

CHAPTER OPENER
'Horribly sublime':
Philip James de
Loutherbourg's
painting 'Coalbrookdale
by Night' (1801)
illustrates both the
magnificence of early
industrial sites and the
violation they wrought
on the landscape.

So now, where Derwent rolls his dusky floods
Through vaulted mountains, and a night of woods,
The nymph, Gossypia, treads the velvet sod,
And warms with rosy smiles the watery god;
His ponderous oars to slender spindles turns,
And pours o'er massy wheels his foamy urns;
With playful charms her hoary lover wins,
And wields his trident, – while the monarch spins.
First with nice eye emerging Naiads cull
From leathery pods the vegetable wool;
With wiry teeth the revolving cards release
The tangled knots, and smooth the ravell'd fleece;
Next moves the iron hand with fingers fine,
Combs the wide card, and forms th'eternal line;
Slow, with soft lips, the whirling can acquires
The tender skeins, and wraps in rising spires;
With quicken'd pace successive rollers move,
And these retain, and those extend the rove.
Then fly the spoles, the rapid axles glow,
And slowly circumvolves the labouring wheel below.

Masson Mill, a few miles from Matlock, survives to this day as a tourist attraction. Its gleaming axles and whirling spools are still redolent with poetry, a sanitised reminder of the high hopes of progress in the early days of machinery powered by water and by steam.

Arthur Young (1741–1820) was an East Anglian farmer. He began his literary career by writing novels, but turned to detailed analysis of agricultural and industrial developments. Touring England in 1770, Young viewed the spectacular iron furnaces of Abraham Darby's Coalbrookdale, in Shropshire, with mixed feelings. He found the 'immense hills' and 'beautiful sheets of hanging wood' of the dale itself intensely romantic, 'too beautiful to be much in unison with that variety of horrors art has spread at the bottom'. Even so, he appreciated the fascination of the site, concluding that 'the noise of the forges and mills and all their vast machinery, the flames bursting from the furnaces with the burning of the coal and the smoke of the lime kilns, are altogether horribly sublime'. At this time 'horrible' was a compliment.

Young wrote at a tipping point in the history of aestheticism: fifteen years later the poet Anna Seward (1747–1809), famous as the 'Swan of Lichfield', would shudder at 'violated Coalbrook', 'Scene of superfluous grace, and wasted bloom' ('Coalbrook Dale', 1785). In 1814 William Wordsworth's poem 'The Excursion' reflected his concern at the encroachment of manufacturing towns on the countryside.

... From the germ
Of some pure hamlet, rapidly produced
Here a huge town, continuous and compact,
Hiding the face of earth for leagues – and there,
Where not a habitation stood before,
Abodes of men irregularly massed
Like trees in forests, – spread through spacious tracts,
O'er which the smoke of unremitting fires
Hangs permanent, and plentiful as wreaths
Of vapour glittering in the morning sun
Even at night, when 'soothing darkness spreads o'er hill and
vale', there is no escape from industry: just as the workers
... issue from the illumined pile,
A fresh band meets them, at the crowded door ...
Enter, and each the wonted task resumes
Within this temple, where is offered up
To Gain, the master idol of the realm,
Perpetual sacrifice.

ABOVE
'The ringing
grooves of change':
J.C. Bourne's 1837
wash-and-ink drawing
of the construction of
a cutting at Park Street,
Camden Town, shows
how dramatically
railways changed
urban landscapes.

RIGHT
Engineering triumphs
such as the viaduct
that carried trains
across the Sankey
Valley on the Liverpool
to Manchester Railway
were popular subjects
for artists. Coloured
lithograph by T.T. Bury,
1831.

46

However, most writers of the time were still awed and impressed by industrial progress. 'The great aqueduct bridge over the deep valley and river of Kelvin, along which the canal connecting the Firths of Forth and Clyde is carried, is one of the most magnificent works of art in Scotland', announced *The Mirror of Literature, Amusement, and Instruction* in 1823. When Thomas Carlyle saw a train for the first time in 1842, he said to his companion, 'These are our poems'. Alfred, Lord Tennyson had already obliged, celebrating the new and powerful tenor of the age. 'Let the great world spin for ever down the ringing grooves of change', he wrote in 'Locksley Hall' (1835).

In August 1830 the actress and author Fanny Kemble (1809–93) described an excursion on George Stephenson's first 'steam-carriage' with fascinated enthusiasm. 'We were introduced to the little engine which was to drag us along the rails. She (for they make these curious little fire-horses all mares) consisted of a boiler, a stove, a small platform, a bench, and a barrel containing enough water to prevent her from being thirsty for fifteen miles.'

But the death of the financier MP William Huskisson after he fell under the wheels of the Rocket during a stop on its inaugural journey from Liverpool to Manchester on 15 September 1830 confirmed the worst fears of those who believed railway lines ruined the landscape and threatened local communities and cottage industry. When Fanny Kemble recorded the arrival of the Rocket in Manchester, she described how, high above the scowling crowd of mechanics and artisans, gathered to protest against the scheme, 'a loom had been raised, at which sat a tattered, starved-looking weaver, evidently set there as a representative man, to protest against this triumph of machinery and the gain and glory which wealthy Liverpool and Manchester would derive from it' (*Record of a Girlhood*, 1878).

Deeply depressed at the advance of the railway into his beloved Lake District, Wordsworth penned the splendid sonnet 'Proud were ye, Mountains' (1844), criticising the 'Thirst for Gold' which had led to the building of the Kendal to Windermere railway. A year later, when the line to Barrow was being built, he wrote 'At Furness Abbey'.

> Well have yon Railway Labourers to THIS ground
> Withdrawn for noontide rest. They sit, they walk
> Among the Ruins, but no idle talk
> Is heard; to grave demeanour all are bound;
> And from one voice a Hymn with tuneful sounds
> Hallows once more the long-deserted Quire
> And thrill the old sepulchral earth, around.
> Others look up. And with fixed eyes admire
> That wide-spanned arch, wondering how it was raised,
> To keep, so high in air, its strength and grace:
> All seem to feel the spirit of the place,
> And by the general reverence God is praised.
> Profane Despoilers, stand ye not reproved,
> While thus these simple-hearted men are moved?

In 1870, when the geologist Adam Sedgwick revisited Furness, which he had known in the 1820s when 'all was silence and solitude', he passed Furness Abbey on the train. Across Morecambe Bay was Barrow, where 'we saw gigantic furnaces sending into the sky a vapour so dark, that it seemed to come from the nostrils of Satan ... all around us smelt of fire and brimstone.' A similarly half-admiring vision of industrial 'pandaemonium' by Richard Jefferies described his visit to the Swindon railway works in 1867. 'Here is a vast wilderness – an endless vista of forges glaring with blue flames ... far ahead sparks fly in showers from the tortured anvils high in the air, looking like minute meteors. This place is a temple to Vulcan.'

George Eliot was the pen-name of Mary Ann Evans (1819–80). She grew up, and set most of her novels, in Warwickshire, which she described as 'fat, central England', full of buttercups, tree-studded hedgerows and elms. *The Mill on the Floss* (1860) offers lyrical descriptions of childhood haunts, 'the great chestnut tree under which they played at houses, their own little river, the Ripple, where the banks seemed like home'. As the industrial revolution encroached, the young Eliot saw smoke rising from the ever-encroaching coal-mining, pot-holed lanes scoured out into tarmac roads, and armies of Irish navvies hacking into the earth to build canals and railways. The local villagers began to leave the fields to work in the pits; those who remained struggled to pay the exorbitant rents demanded of tenant farmers. All this was in striking contrast to the wealth and elegance of Arbury Hall, where, because her father was the estate's manager, she was allowed to use the library.

Eliot was no backward-looking romantic; she had a sharp eye for agricultural mismanagement, and her greatest novel *Middlemarch, A Study of Provincial Life* (1872) looked hopefully to the future. Its heroine Dorothea puts aside personal misery to engage with a wider world beyond herself; she sees people going to work in the early morning, and 'feels the largeness of the world and the manifold wakings of men to labour and endurance knitted together'. Set in 1832, when towns such as Coventry (on which *Middlemarch* is based) were expanding and railway lines were carving their relentless way across the landscape, it accurately reflected provincial belief that no good was likely to come to them personally from any of these changes. When a line is planned through Lowick, 'where the cattle had hitherto grazed in a peace unbroken by astonishment', the avaricious and wealthy Mrs Waule predicts to her brother Peter Featherstone that 'The cows will all cast their calves'. He, however, foresees a tidy profit in first obstructing and then allowing a railway line. By contrast, Hiram the waggoner fears that 'there'll be no stirring from one place to another', and believes that teams of horses will disappear. He and a band of smock-frocked labourers attack a railway surveying party; Caleb Garth, the epitome of wisdom and acceptance in the novel, calms down the little mob. 'Somebody told you the railroad was a bad thing. That was a lie. It may do a little harm here and there, to this and that; and so does the sun in heaven. But the railway's a good thing.' 'Good for the big folks to make money out on', ripostes a labourer, unconvinced.

Dark Satanic Mills

The glamour of the first industrial landscapes soon became tarnished, and by the middle of the nineteenth century the appalling conditions in sprawling cotton industry conurbations in the north of England were the subject of widespread concern. Many novelists pointed up the contrast between the impressive architecture and magnificent engineering and the human misery of the men, women and children who slaved at the machines.

Charlotte Brontë's *Shirley* was written in 1849, but it was set in the early years of the century, when English manufacturers were suffering during the Napoleonic wars. She warned that it was to be 'something unromantic as a Monday morning ... cold lentils and vinegar without oil'. Set among the Yorkshire textile mills, the novel's highly original heroine is the beautiful and proudly independent Shirley Keeldar. An heiress, she loves pacing the moors and plans to picnic and paint with her friend Caroline Helstone in Nunnwood, the ancient forest close to Fieldhead,

OPPOSITE
The manuscript of George Eliot's *Middlemarch* (1872), showing the scene where Caleb warns the would-be trainwreckers that they risked 'handcuffs and the Middlemarch jail'.

"Aw!" was the answer, dropped at intervals by each according to his degree of uneasiness.

"Nonsense! No such thing! They're looking out to see which way the railroad is to take. Now, my lads, you can't hinder the railroad: it'll be made whether you like it or not. And if you go fighting against it, you'll get yourselves into trouble. The law gives those men leave to come The owners has nothing to say against it. and ~~here.~~ If you meddle with 'em you'll have to do with the constable & Justice Blakesley, & with the handcuffs & Middlemarch jail. And you might be in for it now, if anybody informed against you."

Caleb paused here, & perhaps the greatest orator could not have chosen either his pause or his images better for the occasion.

"But come, you didn't mean any harm. Somebody told you the railroad was a bad thing. That was a lie. It may do a bit of harm and here & there, to this & to that; ~~neither~~ so does the sun in heaven. But the railway's a good thing."

"Aw, good for the big folks to make money out on," said old Timothy Cooper, who had stayed behind turning his hay while

ABOVE
Fanny Trollope's *The Life and Adventures of Michael Armstrong, the Factory Boy* (1840), shocked middle-class readers with descriptions of factory children, here seen eating pig swill in one of Auguste Hervieu's vivid illustrations.

the picturesque and ancient home of Keeldar's family for many generations. She is equally interested in manufacturing and prefers the counting house to her elegant drawing room. Brontë contrasts her ideals with the hard-hearted, half-Dutch tenant of her mill, Robert Moore. Oblivious of the hardships suffered by his workers when he introduces labour-saving machinery, he is incensed with fury when it is destroyed by Luddites. All is finally resolved when Robert abandons his avaricious plan to marry Shirley and follows his heart by marrying the portionless Caroline, while Shirley at last admits her own love for his brother Louis, her one-time tutor. The old mill is pulled down and a fine new one built, surrounded by model housing and schools for both the workers and 'the houseless, the starving and the unemployed'.

The Life and Adventures of Michael Armstrong, the Factory Boy (1840) was written by Mrs Fanny Trollope (1779–1863), whose son Anthony would follow in her footsteps as a best-selling writer. Mrs Trollope then rivalled Charles Dickens in popularity, and was acclaimed for the biting satire and wit of both her travel writings and her novels. When she read *Robert Blincoe, A Memoir* (1832) – the true story of a boy brought up in the St Pancras workhouse, then sold on to a Lancashire cotton-mill – she went to look at conditions there herself; they inspired her to write *Michael Armstrong*, a damning exposé of the use and maltreatment of children in factories. The resulting tale was the harder-hitting because of the lively engravings by Auguste Hervieu that illustrated it.

Benjamin Disraeli (1804–81) sympathised with the demands of the 1838 People's Charter for fairer parliaments, and believed that the salvation of the working classes lay in a renewed relationship with the aristocracy. In 1842 he founded the 'Young England' movement, calling for an alliance between the Chartist Radicals and the Tories. He visited Manchester for the first time in 1843, and it appears in idealised form in his novel *Coningsby* (1844). Here the heir to a great estate, Henry Coningsby, also goes north.

He had passed over the plains where iron and coal supersede turf and corn, dingy as the entrance of Hades, and flaming with furnaces; and now he was among illumined factories, with more windows than Italian palaces, and smoking chimneys taller than Egyptian obelisks.

Disraeli described well-run factories and mills, and concluded that 'Rightly understood, Manchester is as great a human exploit as Athens'. But his novel *Sybil, or The Two Nations* (1845), written after he had read Friedrich Engels' shocking *Condition of the Working Class in England in 1844*, offered an altogether different picture of 'the great metropolis of machinery'.

An infinite populace kept swarming to and fro from the closed courts and pestilential cul-de-sacs that continually communicated with the streets by narrow archways, like the entrances of hives, so low that you were obliged to stoop for admission, while ascending to these same streets from their dank and dismal dwellings by narrow flights of steps, the subterranean nation of the cellars poured forth to enjoy the coolness of the summer night.

Northern industrial towns such as Manchester and Preston were harshly pilloried in Charles Dickens' *Hard Times* (1854), one of the few novels he set outside London. 'Coketown' is 'an ugly citadel where Nature was as strongly bricked out as killing airs and gases were bricked in'.

It was a town of red brick, or of brick that would have been red if the smoke and ashes had allowed it; but as matters stood, it was a town of unnatural red and black like the painted face of a savage. It was a town of machinery and tall chimneys, out of which interminable serpents of smoke trailed themselves for ever and ever, and never got uncoiled. It had a black canal in it, and a river that ran purple with ill-smelling dye, and vast piles of building full of windows where there was a rattling and a trembling all day long, and where the piston of the steam-engine worked monotonously up and down, like the head of an elephant in a state of melancholy madness. It contained several large streets all very like one another, and many small streets still more like one another, inhabited by people equally like one another, who all went in and out at the same hours, with the same sound upon the same pavements, to do the same work, and to whom every day was the same as yesterday and to-morrow, and every year the counterpart of the last and the next.

Dickens was critical of the Utilitarian philosophy that lay behind both the grasping meanness of employers such as Bounderby and working-class schools such as Mr Gradgrind's, where children were taught only to be 'little parrots and calculating machines'. The conclusion of *Hard Times* is unmitigatedly bleak, with Gradgrind's pupils coming to sad ends; only the circus child Sissy Jupe holds on to the rich world of folk traditions from which she originally came.

Neither Dickens nor Disraeli offered viable solutions to the conditions of the

51

OVERLEAF
Drawings by the Chartist reformer Ernest Jones contrasting an idealised Grecian City with a nightmare vision of a northern English Town, 1848.

working classes, suspicious as they both were of trade unions. Elizabeth Gaskell (1810–65) is best known today for *Cranford* (1855), her humorous and affectionate depiction of Knutsford, the Cheshire town in which she was brought up. Her contemporary reputation, however, was for hard-hitting social realism. She was married to a Unitarian minister with a parish in the heart of Manchester where, as well as bringing up their four daughters, she distributed food and clothes to the poor. 'I had always felt a deep sympathy with the careworn men, who looked as if doomed to struggle through their lives in strange alternations between work and want', Gaskell wrote in the preface to her first book, *Mary Barton: A Tale of Manchester Life* (1848). Her powerful descriptions of working-class slums bear witness to personal observation:

> As they passed, women from their doors tossed household slops of EVERY description into the gutter; they ran into the next pool, which overflowed and stagnated. Heaps of ashes were the stepping-stones, on which the passer-by, who cared in the least for cleanliness, took care not to put his foot. Our friends were not dainty, but even they picked their way, till they got to some steps leading down to a small area, where a person standing would have his head about one foot below the level of the street, and might at the same time, without the least motion of his body, touch the window of the cellar and the damp muddy wall right opposite. You went down one step even from the foul area into the cellar in which a family of human beings lived. It was very dark inside. The window-panes, many of them, were broken and stuffed with rags, which was reason enough for the dusky light that pervaded the place even at midday. After the account I have given of the state of the street, no one can be surprised that on going into the cellar inhabited by Davenport, the smell was so foetid as almost to knock the two men down. Quickly recovering themselves, as those inured to such things do, they began to penetrate the thick darkness of the place, and to see three or four little children rolling on the damp, nay wet brick floor, through which the stagnant, filthy moisture of the street oozed up; the fire-place was empty and black; the wife sat on her husband's lair, and cried in the dark loneliness.

In *North and South* (1855), Mrs Gaskell takes her heroine Margaret Hale from a pretty Hampshire town to 'Milton', yet another highly critical portrait of Manchester.

> For several miles before they reached Milton, they saw a deep lead-coloured cloud hanging over the horizon in the direction in which it lay. It was all the darker from contrast with the pale grey-blue of the wintry sky; for in Heston there had been the earliest signs of frost. Nearer to the town, the air

had a faint taste and smell of smoke; perhaps, after all, more a loss of the fragrance of grass and herbage than any positive taste or smell. Quick they were whirled over long, straight, hopeless streets of regularly-built houses, all small and of brick. Here and there a great oblong many-windowed factory stood up, like a hen among her chickens, puffing out black 'unparliamentary' smoke ...

Margaret is both attracted and repelled by the mill-owner, John Thornton. She sympathises far more with the working-class Higgins family, appreciating the argument that trade unions are the only way that the workers can get a fair deal. The violent strike scene, in which Margaret shames the mob who are about to attack John Thornton, owed much to the strike of Preston millworkers in 1853–4; the duration and intensity of this dispute shocked middle-class opinion. Gaskell's vision of a

ABOVE
Manchester from Kersal Moor by William Wylde, 1857. Margaret Hale sees just such a scene on approaching 'Milton', the fictional setting of Elizabeth Gaskell's *North and South* (1855).

ABOVE
Engraving from *The Illustrated London News* of December 1853 showing George Cowell addressing workers at the start of the Preston Lock Out. This lasted until May 1854, and is paralleled in the strike and lock-out in Elizabeth Gaskell's *North and South*.

woman appealing to a mob's better nature is similar to Disraeli's scene in *Sybil*, when the squire's wife invites rioters into her gardens and feeds them.

A more optimistic view of industrial development was offered by the many tales that the prolific author Arnold Bennett (1867–1931) set in the urban sprawl of the Staffordshire potteries, 'five contiguous towns, whose red-brown bricks have inundated the moorland like a succession of great lakes strung along by some St Lawrence of a main road'. *The Card* (1911), the story of the rise of Denry Machin from seamstress's son to Mayor of 'Bursley', is a playful portrait of his ebullient young self. When Bennett describes the slopstone and antique crockery, the unlit fire and the pump in the street of the tiny slum dwelling in 'Chapel Alley' where Machin collects the rent from Mrs Hullins, 'the last old woman in Bursley to smoke a cutty [clay pipe]', we sense that he knew such places and such women well. He makes it clear that the new dwellings that were springing up everywhere are great improvements on the old.

Better known, and fascinating both in its realism and drawing of the 'new women' of his age, is Bennett's *Clayhanger* series; many of its locations are still recognisable today in Burslem. *Clayhanger* (1910) begins the story of Edwin Clayhanger, a young man who wants to be an architect, but philosophically submits to his father's insistence that he go into the family printing business. His one small rebellion is to choose to marry Hilda Lessways, an independent-minded woman from the south. *Hilda Lessways* (1911) covers the same period of time seen from Hilda's point of view, and reveals her unhappy past. *These Twain* (1916) shows them struggling to reconcile their incompatibilities as a couple, together but also apart, while *The Roll-Call* (1918) is the story of the unattractively arrogant George, Hilda's son by her first marriage. George brazenly leeches off Edwin's wealth, reflecting Bennett's belief that financial hardship in youth is better for the character than easy wealth.

Bennett's novels are almost cinematic in their depiction of the changing face of the five towns in the last decade of the nineteenth century. In the opening scene of *Clayhanger* the landscape is vividly realised:

OPPOSITE
Opening page of the manuscript of Arnold Bennett's delightful comic novel about the potteries *The Card* (1911), which he originally called *The Deeds of Denry the Audacious*.

THE DEEDS OF DENRY THE AUDACIOUS
by Arnold Bennett

DEED I. THE DANCE
~~THE DANCE~~

How he educated himself

Edward Henry Machin ~~was born~~ first saw the smoke on the 27th. May 1867, in Brougham Street, Bursley, the most ancient of the Five Towns. Brougham Street runs down ~~south~~ from St Luke's Square, ~~and consists~~ partly of straight into the Shropshire Union Canal, and consists partly of buildings known as "potbanks" (until they come to be sold by auction, when auctioneers describe them as "extensive earthenware ~~manufactur~~ manufactories") and partly of cottages whose highest rent is four-and-six a week. In such surroundings was an extraordinary man born. He was the only anxiety of a widowed mother, who gained her livelihood and his by making up 'ladies' own materials' in ladies' own houses. Mrs. Machin, however, had a specialty apart from her vocation; she could wash flannel ~~without~~ ~~shrinking~~ with less shrinking than any other woman in the district, and she could wash fine lace without ruining it; thus often she came to sew and remained to wash. A somewhat gloomy woman; thin, with a tongue! But I liked her. She saved a certain amount of time every day by addressing her son as Denry instead of Edward Henry.

Not intellectual, not industrious, Denry would have ~~o~~ maintained the average dignity of labour on a potbank had he not at the age of twelve won a scholarship from the Board School to the Endowed ~~Middle~~ School. He owed his ~~bron~~ triumph to audacity rather than learning, and to chance rather than design. On the second day of the examination he happened to arrive in the examination-room ten minutes too soon for the afternoon sitting. He wandered about the place exercising his curiosity, and reached the master's desk. On the desk was a tabulated form with names of candidates and the number of marks achieved by each in each subject of the previous day. He had done badly in geography, and saw seven ~~geograp~~ marks against his name in the geographical column, out of a possible thirty. The figures had been written in pencil. The very pencil lay on the desk. He picked it up, and at the rows of empty desks; glanced at the door, and wrote a neat "2" in front of the ~~seven~~; then he strolled innocently forth and ~~arrived late for the~~ came back late. His ~~trick~~ ought to have been found out — the odds were against him — but it was not found out. Of course it was dishonest. Yes, but I will not agree that Denry was uncommonly vicious. ~~So~~ Every schoolboy is dishonest, by the adult standard. If I knew an honest schoolboy I would begin to count my silver spoons as he grew up. All is fair between schoolboys and schoolmasters.

ABOVE
Engine shaft at The
406, Cook's Kitchen
Mine, Cornwall.
Photograph by
J.C. Burrows, 1893.
Burrows' photographs
provided an insight
into the working
conditions of miners
in the late nineteenth
century and were
greatly enhanced by
the development of
flashlight techniques.

Edwin Clayhanger stood on the steep-sloping, red-bricked canal bridge, in the valley between Bursley and its suburb Hillport. In that neighbourhood the Knype and Mersey canal formed the western boundary of the industrialization of the Five Towns. To the east rose pitheads, chimneys, and kilns, tier above tier, dim in their own mists. To the west, Hillport Fields, grimed but possessing authentic hedgerows, and winding paths, mounted broadly up to the sharp ridge on which stood Hillport Church, a landmark. Beyond the ridge, and partly protected by it from the driving smoke of the Five Towns, lay the fine and ancient Tory borough of Oldcastle.

Towards the end of *These Twain*, two decades later, Edwin crosses the same bridge and thinks about how both his life and the potteries have changed. 'Below and around the Church clock the vague fires of Cauldon Bar Ironworks played, and the tremendous respiration of the blast-furnaces filled the evening.' Walking home to the once prestigious suburb to which they moved when he became successful, 'he went by all the new little streets of cottages with drawing-rooms ... These mysterious newcoming families from nowhere were driving him out.' Hilda wants to move to Ladderedge Hall, 'seat of the Beechinors for about a hundred years ('"Seat', eh!", Edwin murmured sarcastically)', a country house, half an hour away from the busy potteries. Regretful at moving but proud of his wealth, Edwin will agree to go.

Caverns of Night

Mining for useful minerals is almost as old as England, and its inevitable dangers have attracted a deep loyalty that is well attested in literature. Early mining works were seen as wonders to be admired. In heroic verse John Dalton (1709–63) highlighted 'the glories of the mine' in his 'Descriptive Poem addressed to Two Ladies on their Return from Viewing the Mines near Whitehaven' (1755). In it, he describes how the intrepid Misses Lowther, daughters of the owner of the mines, go deep into the mine, which extended 'thrice Dover's cliff' depth beneath the sea.

> Agape the sooty collier stands,
> His axe suspended in his hands,
> His Ethiopian teeth the while
> Grin horrible a ghastly smile,
> To see two goddesses so fair
> Descend to him from fields of air ...
> Down to the cold and humid caves,
> Where hissing fall the turbid waves.
> Resounding deep thro' glimmering shades,
> The clank of chains your ears invades ...
> Pumps moved by rods from ponderous beams
> Arrest the unsuspecting streams,
> Which soon a sluggish pool would lie;
> Then spout them foaming to the sky.

59

The ladies were fortunate. In 1910 an undersea Whitehaven mine was flooded in Britain's worst mining disaster, killing 136 miners.

Although there were many factual reports on the worsening conditions in the intensively worked nineteenth-century collieries, there was no British equivalent of Emile Zola's great mining novel *Germinal* (1885) until D.H. Lawrence (1885–1930) wrote *Sons and Lovers* (1913). Lawrence's purpose was less political and more passionate and idealistic than Zola's tale of brutalities, anarchism and sabotage. It is first and foremost a study of family relationships and unsuccessful love affairs, but it draws on his own experiences growing up in the Nottinghamshire mining village of Eastwood. In a 1929 essay, 'Nottinghamshire & The Mining Countryside', he described Eastwood as 'a queer jumble of the old England and the new', where 'life was a curious cross between industrialism and the old agricultural England of Shakespeare and Milton and Fielding and George Eliot'. He went on to romanticise the intimacy of the male mining community. 'The miners worked underground as a sort of intimate community, they knew each other practically naked, and with curious close intimacy, and the darkness and the underground and intuitional contact between the men

very highly developed.' Out of the pit, the men returned to country ways, foraging, poaching and fishing. 'The real tragedy of England, as I see it, is the tragedy of ugliness. The country is so lovely: the man-made England so vile. I know that the ordinary collier, when I was a boy, had a peculiar sense of beauty, coming from his intuitive and instinctive consciousness'. He concluded, 'the human soul needs actual beauty even more than bread ... It is far more deep in the men than in the women'.

How Green Was My Valley (1939), Richard Llewellyn's best-selling novel about a mining community in Victorian times, was an homage to his roots. Llewellyn (1906–83), the Hendon-born son of Welsh parents, spent long summer holidays with his grandfather in the Rhondda valley mining community of Gilfach Goch, in Glamorganshire. Apart from this he spent very little time in Wales, gathering the facts for his novel by talking to mining families in South Wales and researching mining history. Two of the novel's sequels take the hero Huw Morgan to Argentina and the fourth, *Green, Green My Valley Now* (1975), sees him return to Wales.

Other 1930s novels about mining communities were written from bitter experience of the years of the Great Depression. Walter Brierley (1900–72) was a Derbyshire miner who vividly conveyed both the terrifying dangers of the pit and the humiliation of claiming benefits. In the lay-offs of the 1930s, 'the general tone was one of aimlessness – of men decaying. One day you would move along with a man, the next ... he would not be there; somebody would say they had fetched him out of the canal the night before.' His first novel, *Means Test Man* (1935), explained that 'it was something else beside a means test, it tested one's soul ... However far back into oneself one retreated, still the test followed, measuring, measuring.' In a passage in his next book, *Sandwichman*, the hero, on a day release university course as Brierley had been, studies Latin and Logic underground by the light of his lamp while taking a break from hacking at coal.

Lewis Jones (1897–1939), a committed communist, was chairman of the Cambrian Lodge of the South Wales Miners Federation. Refusing to work with 'scab' labour, he resigned from his job in the Nottinghamshire coalfields in 1929 and remained unemployed for the rest of his life. His novels *Cwmardy* (1937) and *We Live* (1939) are true-to-life descriptions of the crisis of masculinity experienced in mining communities as unemployment bit deep. Harold Heslop (1898–1983), who worked for many years at Harton Colliery, South Shields, had a varied and extensive experience of collieries in the north of England. Such novels as *Last Cage Down* (1935) and *The Earth Beneath* (1946) conjure up both the grandeur and the peril of mining processes. His description of the beehive coke ovens is reminiscent of the first awed chroniclers of the industrial scene.

OPPOSITE
Still from the 1941 film by John Ford of Richard Llewellyn's classic account of a Welsh mining community, *How Green Was My Valley* (1939).

BELOW
Front cover of Walter Brierley's searing account of miners' hardships during the Depression, *Means Test Man* (1935).

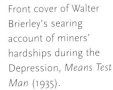

61

When these contraptions were set ablaze, they tore the darkness out of the
moonless nights, and flung the surrounding countryside into a ruddy glow,
which hung aloft as a sulphurous visitation.

Much influenced by D.H. Lawrence and Zola, J.C. Grant's *The Back-to-Backs* (1930) rivalled
Mary Webb's purple prose in his descriptions of life in the mining communities.

Like the mayflies of the swamps, men and women burst from the whole
slime of primeval passion, fluttered for a spasm of time on hopeless ludicrous
wings, and sank back at last into the black slime of civilized passion –
white, black and white, coally flesh and white flesh, darkness and light then
blackness forever ...

The children grew into the pit as they grew into breeches. Their going was
as sure as sunrise, certain as death. The buzzer blew for all alike – reveille,
lights out, the last post.

Urban Modernism

During the Depression years between the two World Wars, industries and businesses struggled to re-establish themselves. Writers and poets were torn between admiration and dislike of 'modernism' – brash, functional and dauntingly foreign, deriving as it did from both the German Bauhaus movement and America's boom economy. Stephen Spender and W.H. Auden, Aldous Huxley and D.H. Lawrence, Evelyn Waugh and George Orwell looked at the new Britain with jaundiced eyes.

George Orwell (1903–50) wrote *The Road to Wigan Pier* (1937) after spending two wintry months living with working people in Wigan, Barnsley and Sheffield. His stay was to fulfil a commission to write a documentary account of the living conditions of unemployed workers in the north for the Left Book Club, and the result was a searing picture of squalor and human misery.

BELOW
George Orwell spent several months living among unemployed working people to research his harrowing account of their lives: this is his own unemployment book for 1933–34, registered to his real name, Eric Blair.

The train bore me away, through the monstrous scenery of slag-heaps, chimneys, piled scrap-iron, foul canals, paths of cindery mud criss-crossed by the prints of clogs. This was March, but the weather had been horribly cold and everywhere there were mounds of blackened snow. As we moved slowly through the outskirts of the town we passed row after row of little grey slum houses running at right angles to the embankment. At the back of one of the houses a young woman was kneeling on the stones, poking a stick up the leaden waste-pipe which ran from the sink inside and which I suppose was blocked. I had time to see everything about her – her sacking apron, her clumsy clogs, her arms reddened by the cold. She looked up as the train passed, and I was almost near enough to catch her eye. She had a round pale face, the usual exhausted face of the slum girl who is twenty-five and looks forty, thanks to miscarriages and drudgery; and it wore, for the second in which I saw it, the most desolate, hopeless expression I have ever seen. It struck me then that we are mistaken when we say that 'it isn't the same for them as it would be for us', and that people bred in the slums can imagine nothing but the slums. For what I saw in her face was not the ignorant suffering of an animal. She knew well enough what was happening to her – understood as well as I did how dreadful a destiny it was to be kneeling there in the bitter cold, on the slimy stones of a slum backyard, poking a stick up a foul drain-pipe.

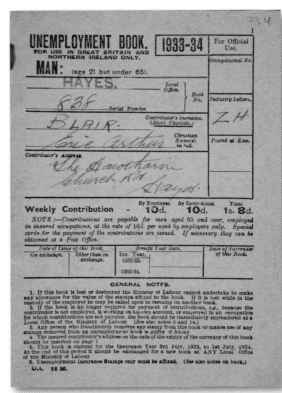

The Road to Wigan Pier might have been calculated to win converts to socialism had not its second half held a profoundly conservative diatribe at the British Socialism of the day. 'One sometimes gets the impression that the mere words "Socialism" and "Communism" draw towards them with magnetic force every fruit-juice drinker, nudist, sandal-wearer, sex maniac, Quaker, "Nature Cure" quack, pacifist and feminist in England.' Orwell went on to condemn Marxism, then at the height of its popularity in Britain, as a 'pea-and-thimble trick with those mysterious entities thesis, anti-thesis and synthesis', and to warn that misplaced admiration for Stalin's 'particularly vicious form of state-capitalism' had led the movement to forget 'that Socialism means justice and common decency'.

Leaving Wigan, Orwell found some grounds for hope as his train entered open country. Here the snow was undefiled and birds were beginning their courting.

> In spite of hard trying, man has not yet succeeded in doing his dirt everywhere. The earth is so vast and still so empty that even in the filthy heart of civilization you find fields where the grass is green instead of grey; perhaps if you looked for them you might even find streams with live fish in them instead of salmon tins. For quite a long time, perhaps another twenty minutes, the train was rolling through open country before the villa-civilization began to close in upon us again, and then the outer slums, and then the slag-heaps, belching chimneys, blast-furnaces, canals, and gasometers of another industrial town.

He reflected that the brief respite seemed 'strange, almost unnatural, as though the open country had been a kind of park'. He concluded pessimistically, 'In a crowded, dirty little country like ours one takes defilement almost for granted. Slag-heaps and chimneys seem a more normal, probable landscape than grass and trees, and even in the depths of the country when you drive your fork into the ground you half expect to lever up a broken bottle or a rusty can.'

Alan Sillitoe (1928–2010) was, like D.H. Lawrence, a native of Nottinghamshire, but his outlook was that of the new era and his writing style closer to the terse modern prose of Orwell and Hemingway. He left school aged 14, working for four years at the Raleigh bicycle factory before joining the Royal Air Force and serving as a wireless operator in Malaya between 1946 and 1949. Like so many of the 'angry young men' of the demobbed generation, and more particularly those too young to serve in the war, Sillitoe found England unsettling and uninspiring, and lived abroad for much of his life. But his love/hate relationship with the world of his youth haunted him, and his most famous books and stories derive from it.

His first novel, *Saturday Night and Sunday Morning* (1958), hit the literary scene like a meteorite from another planet, so compelling was its honesty about the realities of

working-class life. Although it draws upon Sillitoe's own experiences of Nottingham factory life in the 1940s, the novel is set in the much more prosperous 1950s. Televisions gleam in living rooms like alien spaceships and washing machines hum in the scullery; both are paid for on the 'never-never', and jobs, though tediously repetitive, are assured. Social life for the book's anti-hero Arthur is a Saturday night, 'best and bingiest gladtime of the week', when he dons his Teddy suit, gets wasted in the pub, and collapses into the arms of 'lush and loving' Brenda, a friend's obligingly unfaithful wife.

But on Sunday Arthur's favourite pursuit is 'fishing for trout in the cool shade of a willow-sleeved canal near the Balloon Houses, miles away from the city', although the prospect of making love to his mistress in the woods he has known 'since I was

ABOVE
'The camaraderie of factory life': Albert Finney as Arthur and Norman Rossington as Bert in Karel Reisz's 1960 film of Alan Sillitoe's *Saturday Night and Sunday Morning*.

a kid' runs it close. He and Fred look forward to escaping 'beyond the empires of new red-bricked houses' on springtime bicycling trips to 'the fields and woods that rolled on to the Erewash valley and the hills of Derbyshire'.

The book depicts both the relentless demands of the machines and the casual camaraderie of factory life; the mindless and repetitive work combined with the bonus of being able to dream pipe-dreams while you performed it. In the army the only place you had time to think was on the lavatory; at work 'time flew while you wore out the oil-soaked floor and worked furiously without knowing it: you lived in a compatible world of pictures that passed through your mind like a magic lantern, often in vivid and loony-colour, a world where memory and imagination ran free and did acrobatic tricks with your past and with what might be your future, an amok that produced all sorts of agreeable visions'.

By the 1960s much of Britain was revelling in Macmillan's 'never had it so good' years. In Liverpool the Beatles sang with infectious exuberance of *Penny Lane*, and Adrian Henri's 'Mrs Albion You've Got a Lovely Daughter' gave a witty new take on William Blake's 'Daughters of Albion', describing them as

> arriving by underground at Central Station
> eating hot ecclescakes at the Pierhead
> writing 'Billy Blake is fab' on a wall in Mathew St
> taking off their navyblue schooldrawers and
> putting on nylon panties ready for the night.

Prosperity blunted the edge of protest; writers became inward- rather than outward-looking. Exteriors are made symbolic of psychological developments in Jeanette Winterson's *Oranges Are Not the Only Fruit* (1985). Winterson (b.1959) maps her own development by knitting a web of unconventional interpretations of fairytales and myths around the mundane realities of her childhood in Accrington, adopted by a Pentecostal couple who think she is the Chosen One of God, and plan her future as an African missionary.

> We lived in a town stolen from the valleys, a huddled place full of chimneys and little shops and back-to-back houses with no gardens. The hills surrounded us, and our own swept out into the Pennines, broken now and then with a farm or a relic from the war. There used to be a lot of old tanks but the council took them away ... When you climb to the top of the hill and look down you can see everything, just like Jesus on the pinnacle except it's not very tempting ...
> We stood on the hill and my mother said, 'This world is full of sin.'
> We stood on the hill and my mother said, 'You can change the world.'

66

Novels made particular landscapes and cities part of their story as well as their background. David Lodge's *Nice Work* (1988) contrasts a Birmingham car factory with its new university; Pat Barker's early novels *Union Street* (1982), *Blow Your House Down* (1984) and *The Century's Daughter* (1986, later called *Liza's England*) are frank and unsentimental accounts of the often sordid lives of working-class women in the north in the 1970s.

Poems also reflected urban experience. In a striking literary conceit, Ciaran Carson's poem 'Belfast Confetti' (1990) has a bomb loaded with assorted metals explode in a Belfast street during the Troubles. It goes on to offer an ironic catalogue of streets in the city named after long-ago Imperial victories.

> Nuts, bolts, nails, car-keys. A fount of broken type. And the explosion,
> Itself – an asterisk on the map. This hyphenated line, a burst of rapid fire …
> I was trying to complete a sentence in my head but it kept stuttering.
> All the alleyways and side streets blocked with stops and colons.
> I know this labyrinth so well – Balaclava, Raglan, Inkerman, Odessa Street –
> Why can't I escape? Every move is punctuated. Crimean Street. Dead end again.

Carson's poetry has been described by the critic Alan Gillis as 'meta-cartography'. He likens maps to stories. 'A map won't show you exactly how it is, a map is only a schemata of the thing.' In 'Turn Again' (1990) Carson explored the hidden history and present fragility of his home city. 'There is a map of the city which shows the bridge that was never built,/A map which shows the bridge that collapsed; the streets that never existed', it begins, ending with the lament that 'Today's plan is already yesterday's – the streets that were there are gone.'

Industrial Nostalgia

W.H. Auden (1907–73) began taking family holidays in what he later called his Pennine 'Mutterland' at the age of 12. 'To this day Crewe Junction marks the wildly exciting frontier where the alien South ends and the North, my world, begins', he wrote in a 1947 article for *House and Garden* called 'I Like It Cold'. He had been fascinated by lead-mining machinery even earlier in life, when he visited the Blue John Mine at Castleton, near Sheffield. In 1919, discovering the remote and decaying mining village of Rookhope, in Weardale, 'the most wonderfully desolate of all the dales', aroused a vision of Eden betrayed that has Wordsworthian intensity. 'In Rookhope I was first aware / Of Self and not-self, / Death and Dread: / Adits were entrances which led / Down to the Outlawed, the Others, / The terrible, the Merciful, the Mothers' ('New Year Letter', 1941).

In the early 1920s Auden explored mines in the Lake District with his geologist brother John. By then designing imaginary mines had become something of a hobby of his, and he had acquired Thomas Sopwith's *Account of the Mining Districts of Alston*

Names

Soughs?	Veins	Levels or Shafts
May...	Dutton Rake	Smithy Coe
Stoke	Bacchus Pipe	Science
Moorwood	tie the end vein	Broad meadow Engine
Hillcar	Moss R.	Crash purse
Marchill's.	Chapmaiten R.	Shining Cloud
Shining	Tideslow V.	Crookes Drifts
Yatestoop	Pearson's venture. V	Russel's D
Hannaage	Hubnet.	Curry's cross-cut.
Meerhook.	Pyenest	
	Old Master's P.	
	Dinch's R.	
	Amelia Coldberry.	
	Barbara Lott	
	Friardale Hush.	
	Reformer's vein	
	Legrew's - Palfrey	
	Horse butloch V V.	
	Blubber	
	Fluffy V	
	Leonie's hush.	
	Motely Flat.	

Moor, Weardale and Teesdale (1833). During his many years in America, Auden had an Ordnance Survey map of Alston Moor, his favourite place in the world, on his wall.

He described mining locations specifically in his first poems and used metaphors from mining in innumerable later ones. In his 'Letter to Lord Byron' (1937), Auden wrote

> Tramlines and slagheaps, pieces of machinery,
> That was, and still is, my ideal scenery ...
> And from my sixth until my sixteenth year
> I thought myself a mining engineer.
> The mine I always pictured was for lead,
> Though copper mines might, *faute de mieux*, be sound.
> Today I like a weight upon my bed;
> I always travel by the underground.

In 1935 he wrote a verse commentary to John Grierson's mining documentary *Coal Face*.

A powerful poetic portrait of the slow death of industry in the once prosperous and bustling Upper Calder Valley, just west of Halifax, is given by Ted Hughes (1930–98) in his *Remains of Elmet* (1979), in which his words are starkly complemented by Fay Godwin's sombre and elegiac photographs. Hughes, who trained as an archaeologist at Cambridge, called the Calder Valley 'a cradle of the textile industry'. It was also his own: he was born at No. 1, Aspinall St, Mytholmroyd. 'My first six years shaped everything', Hughes once said, and at least eight of his poems are set in the Aspinall St house. The valley went into decline after its mills closed during the Depression. Hughes' parents moved away from the Calder Valley to South Yorkshire in 1937, but he himself returned there in the late 1960s. Roaming the natural wilderness – tamed by industry in the 1800s but now rampant once again – inspired Hughes to create a poetic tapestry of images: crags and brambles; merciless machines and down-trodden workers; memories of his own childhood and references to Celtic legends of what was once the ancient kingdom of Elmet. By the end only a few stoic hill farmers can make a living there: 'Old faces, old roots,/Indigenous memories,/Flat caps. Polished knobs./On favoured sticks.'

> ... here the leaf-loam silence
> Is old siftings of sewing machines and shuttles,
> And the silence of ant-warfare on pine-needles
> Is like the silence of clogs on cobbles,
> And the beech-tree solemnities
> Muffle much cordite.
> ('Hardcastle Crags')

69

OPPOSITE
W.H. Auden's obsessive interest in mines and mining is apparent from jottings in this notebook probably dating from *c*. 1946–65. Here he has recorded lists of terms connected with the industry. The names in the column on the left are all lead mines in Derbyshire.

Amy Cutler, a researcher of cultural geography, has pointed out that *Remains of Elmet* 'is simultaneously about the present collapse of the valley, which signals the end of that Christian and industrial culture which rose upon the ashes of the Celtic kingdom of Elmet, and about the land re-awakening, with a pagan spirit of nature exercising her rights to the valley again as the mills and chapels crumble'.

The wheel of industrial and urban change has come full circle. Today we once again find aqueducts, canals and railway viaducts picturesque. They are preserved by enthusiasts, and lovingly restored steam engines chuff and whistle along remade branch lines. The Reverend W. Awdry's *Thomas the Tank Engine* stories are now one of the biggest brands in children's literature. Railways were also given new romance in Basil Wright and Harry Watt's GPO documentary *Night Mail* (1936), for which W.H. Auden wrote a verse soundtrack:

> This is the night mail crossing the border
> Bringing the cheque and the postal order,
> Letters for the rich, letters for the poor,
> The shop on the corner and the girl next door.
> Past cotton grass and moorland boulder,
> Shovelling white steam over her shoulder,
> Snorting noisily as she passes
> Silent miles of wind-bent grasses.

In 2009 the poet Sean O'Brien reprised the idea in his atmospheric *Night Train*, a celebration of the relics of the age of steam. His poem 'Fireweed' makes the omnipresent rosebay willow herb, famously spread all over Britain because of its affinity for cinders, a symbol of 'the silence / After the age of the train'.

After London (1885), Richard Jefferies' post-apocalyptic novel set in a future in which London has utterly disappeared, has been followed by countless wistful fantasies of predominantly rural civilisation. *Demos* (1886), George Gissing's vision of an entire northern valley blighted by industry being turned back into a green and pleasant land, is being achieved. Both Coalbrookdale and Masson Mill are now tourist attractions. *In the Pennines*, a series of Simon Armitage poems inspired by the landscape, are being engraved on 'Stanza Stones' in places where walkers will discover them. The poems evoke powerful memories of water's vital part in industrial development. One is incised on one of the hundreds of flagstones from former mill buildings which are now being laid by Bradford Council to protect popular footpaths across the Ilkley moors.

OPPOSITE
'Think often of the silent valley, for the god lives there'. Paved path above Lumbutts, near Todmorden, West Yorkshire: Photograph by Fay Godwin for Ted Hughes' *Remains of Elmet*, 1979.

WILD PLACES

In the 1720s the traveller and writer Daniel Defoe shuddered at the 'unhospitable terror' of Westmorland's 'unpassable mountains'; it was 'a country eminent only for being the wildest, most barren and frightful of any that I have passed over in England, or even in Wales itself' (*A Tour Thro' the Whole Island of Great Britain*, 1726). By the middle of the eighteenth century, however, solitude and mystery were beginning to be sought after rather than feared. Mountains were seen as beautiful and sublime, the handiwork of God rather than the devil, whose name had in previous centuries been attached to the most threatening crags and

CHAPTER OPENER
The Lake District
filled Defoe with
'unspeakable terror',
but for later writers
and visitors its solitude
and mystery were
seen as beautiful and
sublime. Windermere
from Orrest Head,
from James Baker
Pyne's *The English Lake
District*, 1853.

The terror inspired by nature stems from 'exultation, awe and delight rather than dread and loathing', claimed Edmund Burke in his *Enquiry into the Origins of the Sublime and Beautiful* (1757). He believed that the sublime lay not only in what was being observed, but also in the emotions and the imagination of the observer. The American author and philosopher Henry Thoreau expressed the same idea with arresting pungency a century later when he wrote, 'It is vain to dream of a wildness distant from ourselves. There is none such. It is the bog in our brains and bowels, the primitive vigour of Nature in us that inspires that dream' (*Journal*, Aug. 30, 1856).

The Alps were a magnet to eighteenth-century travellers seeking the 'delightful horror' that Burke found in nature's most dramatic manifestations. Horace Walpole and Thomas Gray were among the men of letters who toured Savoy in search of sensation. 'Not a precipice, not a torrent, not a cliff but is pregnant with religion and poetry', observed Gray. Things went a little too far when, as they ascended Mount Cenis, a wolf darted out of the woods and seized Walpole's King Charles spaniel, which had been let out of the chaise for a little exercise. Appalled, Gray commented that perhaps Mount Cenis 'carries the permission mountains have of being frightful too far'. Travellers still preferred to be observers at distance, affected mentally, not physically, by what they encountered.

Towards the end of the eighteenth century, war with France made taking the traditional 'Grand Tour' around Europe difficult. At the same time British roads were improving, leading tourists to begin exploring their own country. In 1746 the final crushing of the Jacobites by 'Butcher' Cumberland at Culloden led to the methodical mapping of the newly conquered territory by cartographers and topographers such as Thomas and Paul Sandby. The latter's tranquil depictions of the hitherto feared Highlands formed part of the propaganda of pacifism, and did much to encourage English tourists to visit Scotland.

Travellers were guided in how they viewed the landscape by the influential painter and writer William Gilpin (1724–1804). A native of Cumberland, his origins helped him to see the aesthetic satisfaction of mountains and the natural landscape. In his *Observations on the River Wye, and several parts of South Wales* (1782), he described the setting of Tintern Abbey:

> The woods, and glades intermixed; the winding of the river; the variety of the ground; the splendid ruin, contrasted with the objects of nature; and the elegant line formed by the summits of the hills, which include the whole; make altogether a very inchanting [sic] piece of scenery.

Gilpin invented a way of measuring landscape according to its suitability as a subject for a painting, a concept that he defined as its 'picturesqueness'. He suggested that tourists should turn their backs on whatever beauty spot he had directed them to,

and view it using a Claud glass. This was a shaded and slightly convex mirror which framed and gave a soft, mellow tone to any 'prospect', endowing it with the orderly elegance of a painting by Claude Lorrain, whose Italianate landscapes were then much admired. Gilpin even suggested that at Tintern Abbey 'a mallet judiciously used' could remove the gable ends that 'hurt the eye with their regularity', noting that they 'are not only disagreeable in themselves but confound the perspective'. Gilpin's obsession with picturesque ruins was quickly satirised, first by Thomas Rowlandson's engravings for William Combe's satirical poem *The Tour of Dr Syntax in Search of the Picturesque* (1812) and later by Jane Austen (1775–1817), both in her *History of England* (1791) – in which she declares that Henry VIII's reason for dissolving the monasteries was to 'leave them to the ruinous depredations of time' so that they could be 'of infinite use to the landscape of England' – and in *Northanger Abbey* (1818), in which the young Catherine Morland listens rapt to Henry Tilney's lecture on the picturesque.

> He talked of foregrounds, distances, and second distances – side-screens and perspectives – lights and shades; and Catherine was so hopeful a scholar that when they gained the top of Beechen Cliff, she voluntarily rejected the whole city of Bath as unworthy to make part of a landscape.

ABOVE
'I'll prose it here, I'll verse it there, And picturesque it everywhere'. Illustration by Thomas Rowlandson for *The Tour of Dr Syntax in Search of the Picturesque* (1812), William Combe's satirical poem on seekers after romantic effects in landscape.

Nor were Gilpin's enthusiasms shared by all his contemporaries. In his 1775 *Journal to the Western Isles*, Dr Johnson remained determinedly oblivious to fine effects. Ranting at the filth, destitution and ugliness of the Hebrides, the author concerned himself most in such evidences of civilisation as the hospitality of the MacDonalds of Armidel.

The approach of William Wordsworth (1770–1850) and his turbulent and passionate friend Samuel Taylor Coleridge (1772–1834) was in stark contrast to the cerebral responses of Walpole, Gray and Gilpin. Immersing themselves physically and emotionally in landscape, the two poets made it into a metaphor for character and feelings. For Wordsworth, 'the meanest flower that blows can give/Thoughts that do often lie too deep for tears.' Like Gilpin, he made a pilgrimage to Tintern Abbey, but he had no thought of criticising its over-regular gable ends. Instead, he listened to 'the still sad music of humanity', and was 'well-pleased to recognise in nature and the language of the sense,/The anchor of my purest thoughts, the nurse,/The guide, the guardian of my heart, and soul/Of all my moral being' ('Tintern Abbey', 1798). In 'The Excursion' (1814), Wordsworth spells out how as a boy

He had small need for books; for many a tale
Traditionary, round the mountains hung,
And many a legend, peopling the dark woods,
Nourished Imagination in her growth,
And gave the Mind that apprehensive power
By which she is made quick to recognise
The moral properties and scope of things.

Wordsworth grew up in Cockermouth, Cumberland, in close alliance with his sister Dorothy. His mother died when he was eight, and he was sent to school first in Hawkshead, then in Penrith. As a young man he travelled in Europe, famously

LEFT
Pugnacious and pragmatic, Dr Johnson remained immune to the fashion for romancing the wilderness. This anonymous engraving of 1786 shows him in his travelling dress.

admiring the revolutionary ideals of the French. In 1795 he met Coleridge in Somerset, and two years later he and Dorothy settled in Alfoxden, a few miles from Coleridge's home at Nether Stowey. The trio physically enveloped themselves in nature, striding out for miles every day, and in 1798 *Lyrical Ballads*, a collection that included both Wordsworth's 'Lines composed a few miles above Tintern Abbey' and Coleridge's 'Rime of the Ancient Mariner', was published.

In *The Prelude* (1850) Wordsworth cast back to his youth for an instance of nature as stern moral guardian. In an 'act of stealth and troubled pleasure', he steals a boat at Ullswater and rows out onto the lake, taking a craggy ridge he can see against the clear and starry sky as a landmark.

RIGHT
'The grim shape towered up': Wordsworth found messages from heaven in the Lakeland mountains. Aquatint of 'Lake Windermere' by Jacob Loutherbourg, from *Picturesque Scenery of England and Wales*, 1805.

She was an elfin pinnace; lustily
I dipp'd my oars into the silent lake ...
When from behind that craggy Steep, till then
The bound of the horizon, a huge Cliff,
As if with voluntary power instinct,
Uprear'd its head: I struck, and struck again,
And, growing still in stature, the grim Shape
Towered up between me and the stars, and still,
For so it seemed, with a purpose of its own
And measured motion like a living Thing,
Strode after me.

The logical mind, acquainted with Ullswater, realises that as you row (necessarily facing backwards) away from the western shore, the higher ridges of Helvellyn would naturally come into view. To Wordsworth's romantic perception, the peaks were a manifestation of heavenly displeasure.

Coleridge, a less reflective and more restless spirit than Wordsworth, was equally passionate in sensibility. Born in Ottery St Mary, Devon, his father died when he was ten and he was sent to a London school – a shock to which he attributed his lifelong insecurity. Wordsworth's influence led him to write splendid nature poems while he was at Nether Stowey. In the pantheistic 'Frost at Midnight', Coleridge hopes that his 'cradled infant' Hartley (named for an Enlightenment philosopher whom he deeply admired) would grow up among 'sea, hill and wood', and ... wander like a breeze

> By lakes and sandy shores, beneath the crags
> Of ancient mountain, and beneath the clouds
> Which image in their bulk both lakes and shores
> And mountain crags; so shalt thou see and hear
> The lovely shapes and sounds intelligible
> Of that eternal language, which thy God
> Utters, who from eternity doth teach
> Himself in all, and all things in himself.

ABOVE
Samuel Taylor Coleridge's sketch-map of the Lake District, made in the notebook he took on his tour of 1802. Keswick and Derwentwater are in the top right-hand corner.

In Xannadù did Cubla Khan
A stately Pleasure-Dome decree;
Where Alph, the sacred River, ran
Thro' Caverns measureless to Man
Down to a sunless Sea.
So twice six miles of fertile ground
With Walls and Towers were compass'd round:
And here were Gardens bright with sinuous Rills
Where blossom'd many an incense-bearing Tree,
And here were Forests ancient as the Hills
Enfolding sunny Spots of Greenery.
But o! that deep romantic Chasm, that slanted
Down a green Hill athwart a cedarn Cover,
A savage Place, as holy and inchanted
As e'er beneath a waning Moon was haunted
By Woman wailing for her Dæmon Lover:
From forth
And from this Chasm with hideous Turmoil seething
As if this Earth in fast thick Pants were breathing,
A mighty Fountain momently was forc'd,
Amid whose swift half-intermitted Burst
Huge Fragments vaulted like rebounding Hail,
Or chaffy Grain beneath the Thresher's Flail:
And mid these dancing Rocks at once & ever
It flung up momently the sacred River.
Five miles meandring with a mazy Motion
Thro' Wood and Dale the sacred River

Wordsworth and Dorothy returned to the Lake District in December 1799, establishing themselves at Dove Cottage, near Grasmere. Coleridge followed them in 1800, settling with his family in Keswick, on the shores of Derwentwater. In 1816 he published two unfinished poems, 'Christabel' and 'Kubla Khan'. 'Christabel', described by Coleridge as attempting 'the thing most difficult in the whole field of romance: witchery by daylight', was influenced by the medieval ballads in Thomas Percy's *Reliques of Ancient English Poetry* and Scott's *Lady of the Lake*. It is laced with Lakeland allusions: as the enchantress has her way with Christabel, the matins bell echoes 'in Langdale Pike and Witch's Lair,/And Dungeon Ghyll so foully rent'.

Awesome natural grandeur is made a symbol of mighty power in 'Kubla Khan', a poem which Coleridge claimed came to him suddenly 'in a kind of reverie'. Begun in Nether Stowey and revised in the Lake District, its imagery is the more powerful because it is fantastic; the crags and gullies, rushing rivers and tumbling waterfalls of the Lake District appear distorted out of all proportion – perhaps under the influence of the opium-based laudanum cordial to which Coleridge was addicted.

> But oh! That deep romantic chasm which slanted
> Down the green hill athwart a cedarn cover!
> A savage place! As holy and enchanted
> As e'er beneath a waning moon was haunted
> By woman wailing for her demon lover!
> And from this chasm, with ceaseless turmoil seething,
> As if this earth in fast thick pants was breathing,
> A mighty fountain momentarily was forced
> Amid whose swift half-intermitted burst
> Huge fragments vaulted like rebounding hail,
> Of chaffy grain beneath the thresher's flail:
> And 'mid these dancing rocks at once and ever
> It flung up momently the sacred river.

Coleridge had already applied similar hyperbole to real places in the Lake District. After a long hike in 1802 he wrote an ecstatic description of Moss Force, a waterfall in the Newlands Pass, above Buttermere village. 'What a sight it is to look down on such a Cataract! The wheels, that circumvolve it, the leaping up and plunging forward of that infinity of Pearls and Glass Bulbs, the continual *change* of the *Matter*, the perpetual *Sameness* of the *Form* – it is an awful Image and Shadow of God and the World.'

The diaries that Dorothy Wordsworth kept both at Alfoxden and Grasmere reveal her own close affinity with nature, as well as her deep love for William, 'my Beloved'. At Grasmere she fished, sailed and walked with him, picking up the jottings

OPPOSITE
Opening page of the manuscript of Samuel Taylor Coleridge's unfinished poem 'Kubla Khan', 1816. Although begun in Somerset and set in Xanadu, its 'deep romantic chasms' and 'mighty fountains' echoed the dramatic effects that Coleridge found in Cumbria's mountains and waterfalls.

I wandered lonely as a Cloud
That floats on high oer Vales and Hills
When all at once I saw a crowd
A host of dancing Daffodils;
Along the Lake beneath the trees
Ten thousand dancing in the breeze.

The Waves beside them danced, but they
Outdid the sparkling Waves in glee:—
A Poet could not but be gay
In such a laughing company:
I gaz'd — and gaz'd — but little thought
What wealth the shew to me had brought.

For oft when on my couch I lie
In vacant, or in pensive mood,
They flash upon that inward eye
Which is the bliss of solitude
And then my heart with pleasure fills,
And dances with the Daffodils.

for poems that he often carelessly dropped. Her diaries describe the changing weather and light on the sea, the hills, the lakes and the mountains with a fastidious eye for variation of effect. 'The withered leaves danced with the hailstones ... moonshine like herrings in the water ... I never saw daffodils so beautiful, they tossed & reeled & danced & seemed as if they verily laughed with the wind that blew upon them over the lake.' William is known to have used her daily jottings as inspiration for poems, picking up on those withered leaves in 'A Whirl-blast from Behind the Hill', and on the tossing daffodils in 'I Wandered Lonely as a Cloud'. He likened Dorothy to a 'violet, hidden by a stone', and acknowledged his debt to her in *The Prelude*. 'She, in the midst of all, preserved me still / A Poet, made me seek beneath that name, / And that alone, my office upon earth.' Coleridge also thought Dorothy remarkable: 'her taste a perfect electrometer – it bends, protrudes and draws in at subtlest beauties and most recondite faults'.

'Solitude' (1816), the first poem published by John Keats (1795–1821), is suffused with his longing to escape 'the jumbled heap of murky buildings' and 'climb ... the steep, Nature's Observatory'. Two years later, he went for a walking tour from Lancaster to John o' Groats. The experience provided inspiration for his poem 'Happy is England' and the sublime imagery of 'Hyperion' (1819), in which the sombre stasis of Saturn's lair is juxtaposed with the gossamer delicacy of a dandelion fleece, epitome of an English summer.

83

> Deep in the shady sadness of a Vale,
> Far sunken from the healthy breath of Morn,
> Far from the fiery noon, and Eve's one star,
> Sat grey-hair'd Saturn quiet as a stone,
> Still as the silence round about his Lair.
> Forest on forest hung above his head
> Like Cloud on Cloud. No stir of air was there,
> Not so much life as on a summer's day
> Robs not at all the dandelion's fleece ...

Sydney, Lady Morgan (1781–1859) championed her home country in her novel *The Wild Irish Girl* (1806). It is written in the form of letters from Horatio, the son of an Anglo-Irish earl, banished to the family's remote estates in the northwest of Ireland because of his huge debts. Nothing could be wilder or more sublime, and Horatio quotes from Burke when he describes it:

Mountain rising over mountain, swelled like an amphitheatre to those clouds which, faintly tinged with the sun's prelusive beams, and rising from the earthly summits where they had reposed, incorporated with the kindling

aether of a purer atmosphere. All was silent and solitary – a tranquility tinged with terror, a sort of 'delightful horror', breathed on every side ... I pursued my solitary ramble along a steep and trackless path, which wound gradually down towards a great lake, an almost miniature sea, that lay embosom'd amidst those stupendous heights whose rugged forms, now bare, desolate, and barren, now clothed with yellow furze, and creeping underwood, or crowned with mystic forests, appeared towering above my head in endless variety.

He finds a dilapidated castle in which the last Gaelic and Catholic descendants of the Irish kings, displaced by his ancestors in Cromwellian times, live in impoverished elegance. They are the aged Prince of Inismore and his daughter, the learned and beautiful Glorvina, who plays the harp like a seraph and can quote Tasso and Dante. Naturally Horatio falls in love with her, though he dares not disclose his hated name. Irish humour, courtesy to strangers and selfless generosity are much praised, and the moral made by the happy ending is that absentee landlords need to return and appreciate the natural splendours of their estates instead of exploiting them.

Romancing the Wilderness

Caleb Williams (1794), written by William Godwin (father of Mary Shelley, the author of *Frankenstein*), is a powerful plea for social justice; it is also the first of a tradition of thrillers featuring first-person narration and escapes through wild country. 'I bent myself to the conception of a series of adventures of flight and pursuit; the fugitive in perpetual apprehension of being overwhelmed with the worst calamities', observes the hero of this precursor to *Kidnapped*, *The Thirty-Nine Steps* and *Rogue Male*. There is something of Robin Hood about the intrepid leader of a band of thieves with whom Caleb takes refuge, and their semi-ruined stronghold, deep in the most uncouth and unfrequented part of the forest, is encircled with a stagnant moat. Caleb experiences it, however, as 'Elysium' compared to the prison from which he has just escaped. He subsequently flees to Ireland and to Wales, where he describes the 'face of nature' around the remote little town where he ends up as 'wild and romantic'.

The message is that there is sanctuary in the wilderness; whenever Caleb returns to civilisation he is apprehended by agents of the implacable and all-powerful Falkland, whom he will prove is a murderer only after innumerable misfortunes.

The writer who most famously imbued his native land with wild romance in his own time was Sir Walter Scott (1771–1832). Among Scott's many nicknames were 'the Great Bow-Wow', 'Wizard of the North' and 'the Scottish Prospero', and his epic poems and historical novels, set largely in Scotland, sold in phenomenal numbers. Born in Edinburgh, Scott grew up in the Border country, listening fascinated to local storytellers and developing a passion for chivalric romances and history from an early age. He married a French heiress, became a lawyer, and was appointed Deputy-Sheriff of Selkirk in 1799. Writing, however, dominated his life. In 1805 his printer friend James Ballantyne published *The Lay of the Last Minstrel*, which became an instant success. Scott followed this with *The Lady of the Lake* (1810), which brought tourists in thousands to see Loch Katrine and the Trossachs through his romantic filter.

Many novels followed, three-deckers about the wild Border country and the Highlands that

BELOW
The Lady of the Lake (1810), illustrated with engravings after R. Cook. Illustration to Canto IV, Stanza XXI, 'The Tartan Plaid she first decried / And shrieked till all the Rocks replied'.

were snatched hot from the presses. Scott did not just make landscape ineradicably associated with his stories; he changed the way in which anyone with a drop of Scottish blood viewed their own history. Clan tartans and elaborate genealogies were unearthed or invented, and Scotland became synonymous with romance instead of rebellion at even the highest levels of society. Queen Victoria bought Balmoral Castle, appointed a royal piper to play the bagpipes to her, designed her own Victoria tartan and carried Scott's books with her as guidebooks when she toured the Borders, the Trossachs and other parts of Scotland. Novels such as *Ivanhoe* (1819) and *Kenilworth* (1821) mapped England's history in similar romantic vein.

Emily Brontë (1818–48) was an ardent admirer both of Wordsworth, to whom the sisters sent their first volume of poems in 1846, and of Sir Walter Scott. When the Brontë siblings wrote their 'bed-plays' around toy figures, she chose the Isle of Arran as her home and Sir Walter Scott as her 'cheif [sic] man'. Her own writings were close kin to Coleridge's wild, ecstatic outpourings; she was described by her sister Charlotte as 'a solitude-loving raven, no gentle dove'. Emily revealed her personal take on the sublime in a poem she wrote in 1845.

> No coward soul is mine,
> No trembler in the world's storm-troubled sphere:
> I see Heaven's glories shine,
> And faith shines equal, arming me from Fear.

In the hurricane of a novel that is *Wuthering Heights* (1847), Catherine Earnshaw and Heathcliff possess the elemental qualities of myth. Emily Brontë went further even than Thomas Hardy in her identification of landscape and natural things with emotion. Early in the book the visitor Lockwood dreams that a branch knocking against the window is the ice-cold hand of the ghostly Cathy; and the living girl herself tells Nelly Dean that 'whatever our souls are made of, his [Heathcliff's] and mine are the same; and Linton's is as different as a moonbeam from lightning, or frost from fire'. She goes on to liken her affection for Linton to the changeable foliage of a tree, while her immutable love for Heathcliff resembles 'the eternal rocks beneath'. Heathcliff, whose very name emphasises his closeness to nature, also uses harsh images from the natural world; he mutters mockingly to Hareton, the neglected son of his foster brother, 'Now my bonny lad, you are mine! And we'll see if one tree won't grow as crooked as another with the same wind to twist it.'

No-one who has read *Wuthering Heights* can roam the Yorkshire moors on a stormy day without calling to mind scenes from the book. Haworth, the stone parsonage in which the Brontës developed their fantasy games and wrote books and poems, has now become a shrine for pilgrims from all over the world, who set hopefully out on organised tours around the churchyard and across the moors.

LEFT
Fay Godwin's
photograph of
Top Withens, near
Haworth, the ruined
house which is said
to have provided the
inspiration for Emily
Brontë's *Wuthering
Heights*.

But they will not see Cathy, as Heathcliff did, 'in every cloud, in every tree – filling the air at night, and caught by glimpses in every object'. There are in truth no very exact descriptions of landscape in the book, though the contrast between the isolated farmhouse Wuthering Heights, with its primitive kitchen and huge hearth, and the refined furnishings of the drawing-room at Thrushcross Grange, all silver, gold and crimson, is drawn in minute and telling detail.

A pair of poems, both called 'Wuthering Heights', were written in homage to Emily Brontë by the ill-matched but passionately attached couple, Sylvia Plath (1932–63) and Ted Hughes (1930–98). They visited Haworth in 1961, and walked up to the moor. As the poems show, Plath looked inward, Hughes outward – a difference of view that caused both creative and destructive tensions in their relationship. Plath experienced nature as it impacted on her personally.

> The horizons ring me like faggots,
> Tilted and disparate, and always unstable.
> Touched by a match, they might warm me ...
> If I pay the roots of the heather
> Too close attention, they will invite me
> To whiten my bones among them.

joy and analyze the species of pleasure brooding for me in the h
and situation. It was three o'clock; the church bell tolled as I
passed under the belfry; the charm of the hour lay in its appro
approaching dimness; in the low-gliding and pale-beaming sun
I was a mile from Thornfield, in a lane noted for wild roses
summer, for nuts and blackberries in autumn, and even no
possessing a few coral treasures in hips and haws, but whose
best winter delight lay in its utter solitude and leafless repose.
If a breath of air stirred, it made no sound here, for there w
not a holly, not an evergreen to rustle, and the stripped hawtho
and hazel bushes were as still as the white, worn stones which
causewayed the middle of the path. Far and wide, on each sid
there were only fields, where no cattle now browzed, and the littl
brown birds which stirred occasionally in the hedge looked ~~only~~ li
single russet leaves that had forgotten to drop.

This lane inclined up-hill all the way to Hay; having rea
ed the middle, I sat down on a stile which led thence into a field
Gathering my mantle about me and sheltering my hands in my muff
I did not feel the cold, though it froze keenly, as was attested by a
[sheet of ice covering the causeway where a little brooklet, now co

Hughes, keeping himself completely hidden, watches Plath experience the landscape
as a fantastic wilderness, then brings things back to earth and solid reality.

> ... That climb
> A mile beyond expectation, into
> Emily's private Eden. The moor
> Lifted and opened its dark flower
> For you too. That was satisfactory.
> Wilder, maybe, than ever Emily knew it.
> ... It was all
> Novel and exhilarating to you.
> The book becoming a map. Wuthering Heights
> Withering into perspective. We got there
> And it was all gaze. The open moor,
> Gamma rays and decomposing starlight
> Had repossessed it
> With a kind of blackening smoulder. The centuries
> Of door-bolted comfort finally amounted
> To a forsaken quarry.

89

In *Jane Eyre* Charlotte Brontë (1816–55) created a more civilised gothic hero than her
sister's Heathcliff in Mr Rochester. Jane's first encounter with him is nonetheless
threaded with menace, both natural and mythic. She is sitting late in the evening
above Thornfield Hall 'on which the moon cast a hoary gleam, bringing it out distinct
and pale from the woods that, by contrast with the western sky, now seemed a mass
of shadow'. As she listens to the tinkle of the becks,

A rude noise broke on these fine ripplings and whisperings at once so far
away and so clear: a positive tramp, tramp, a metallic clatter, which effaced
the soft wave-wanderings: as, in a picture, the solid mass of a crag, or the
rough boles of a great oak, drawn in dark and strong on the foreground,
efface the aerial distance of azure hill, sunny horizon, and blended clouds
where tint melts into tint ... As this horse approached, and as I watched for it
to appear in the dusk, I remembered certain of Bessie's tales, wherein figured
a North-of-England spirit called a 'Gytrash', which, in the form of a horse,
mule or large dog, haunted solitary ways ... It was very near, but not yet in
sight; when, in addition to the tramp, tramp, I heard a rush under the hedge,
and close down by the hazel stems glided a great dog, whose black and white
colour made him a distinct object against the trees. It was exactly one form of
Bessie's Gytrash – a lion-like creature with long hair and a huge head.

Then she sees that the horse has a rider, and reason overtakes imagination; she rises, scaring the horse, and the rider is thrown. Hastening to help him she sees him clearly in the moonlight: 'a dark face, with stern features and a heavy brow; his eyes and gathered eyebrows looked ireful and thwarted'. Later, Rochester will recall that first meeting, when, just before proposing to Jane, he recalls her appearing out of the darkness like an elf, and her offer of help seeming 'as if a linnet had hopped to my foot and proposed to bear me on its tiny wing'. The switch from menace to endearing helpfulness symbolises what Jane does for Rochester. Similarly the wild moorland that Emily made so fearsome appears benign and supportive when Jane makes the right moral decision by fleeing across it after discovering the existence of Mrs Rochester:

> I touched the heath: it was dry, and yet warm with the heat of the day. I looked at the sky; it was pure: a kindly star twinkled just above the chasm ridge. The dew fell, but with propitious softness; no breeze whispered. Nature seemed to be benign and good ... Tonight, at least, I would be her guest, as I was her child.

R.D. Blackmore's *Lorna Doone: A Romance of Exmoor* (1869) and *Kidnapped* (1886), Robert Louis Stevenson's tale of David Balfour's flight across the heather, remain admired to this day for offering a 'Call of the Wild' as potent as anything by Jack London. When John Rudd struggles at night through the icy black pool and up the 'fearful torrent way' of the waterfall that leads to the Doone's valley, and Davy and Alan Breck flee over 'wild, houseless, mountains' and across 'well-heads of wild rivers' to Rannoch Moor, 'as waste as the sea; only the moorfowl and peewits crying on it', readers thrill to the recreated wildness of such places, and thousands visit them to relive the stories in their imaginations.

The same appeal is contained in the poems of Gerard Manley Hopkins (1844–89), a Jesuit priest whose poetry, published posthumously in 1918, was a century ahead of its time in praising wildness and prophesying the threat to 'Earth, sweet Earth, sweet landscape'. Poems such as 'That Nature is a Heraclitean Fire' and 'God's Grandeur' issue warnings at man's desecration of it. 'In the Valley of the Elwy', 'Penmaen Pool', 'Ribblesdale' and 'Inversnaid' are compelling pen portraits of the fragility of the wild places that symbolised for Hopkins God's grace to man.

> What would the world be, once bereft
> Of wet and of wildness, let them be left
> O let them be left, wildness and wet;
> Long live the weeds and the wilderness yet.
> ('Inversnaid')

Rediscovering the Wild Places

Crow (1966) more than any other of Ted Hughes' poems deals with man's alienation from nature. The first poem he published after three years of retreat following Sylvia Plath's suicide in 1963, it was described by the poet and critic Calvin Bedient as 'the croak of nihilism itself'. Carnivalesque and bizarre, the greedy and violent Crow's songs 'have no music', Hughes explained. Written 'in a super-simple, super-ugly language', they are 'just what he wanted to say without any other consideration'. Part creation epic, part folktale in the Eastern European tradition, Crow's shamanic fantasies of death and dismemberment bear comparison with scenes in J.G. Ballard's novel *Crash*, and it is not irrelevant that both men lost their wives in sudden and terrible circumstances. *Crow* was never quite completed, 'knocked off his perch' as Hughes put it when, six years after Plath's suicide, his partner Assia committed suicide in 1969. Later in life Hughes achieved a calmer state of mind, reflected in such collections as *Moortown* and *River*, which offer an ecological alternative to materialism in observing and preserving natural things. Hughes' journey from alienation from nature to its rediscovery is a progression typical of writers in modern times. Our new concern for ecology, our sense of alarm at the prospect of nature being irrevocably destroyed, is leading the British to value their increasingly elusive wilderness more and more.

Seamus Heaney (b.1939) 'learned that my local County Derry experience, which I had considered archaic and irrelevant to "the modern world", was to be trusted.' Returning, he drives around for a day, recalled in 'The Peninsula' (1966).

RIGHT
A manuscript page from a draft of Ted Hughes' poem 'Crow and the Fool', showing revisions made while he was writing the series published as *Crow* in 1970.

91

> The glazed foreshore and silhouetted log,
> That rock where breakers shredded into rags,
> The leggy birds stilted on their own legs,
> Islands riding themselves out into the fog.

It is not, however, any wild present, but rather the violent and ancient past signalled by relics sunk in peat that preoccupies him. Heaney interprets the Irish psyche in terms of geology and landscape, particularly the bog landscape, enjoying the links between Ireland's Celtic and Norse antecedents. 'Bog' is itself an Irish word meaning

ABOVE
'I stayed for an
hour watching the
mountain's shadow
narrow and lengthen'.
In *Wild Places*, Robert
MacFarlane describes
how the 'low, broken
desert land' of
Rannoch Moor was
crossed by David
Balfour in Robert
Louis Stevenson's
Kidnapped, and how
reliving memories of
walking there helped
a prisoner in a Nazi
concentration camp to
survive.

soft, he explains in the introduction to his *Bog Poems* (1975). 'We called the bog "the moss", a word with Norse origins that was probably carried to Ulster by the Scottish planters.' Heaney sees the bog, and the ancient remains preserved in it, be they elks, or ships, or people, as a kind of memory-bank, 'a dark casket where we have found many clues to our past and to our cultural identity'. It looks backwards into history, rather than forward towards progress. 'I step through origins / Like a dog turning / Its memories of wilderness / On the kitchen mat', he writes in 'Kinship'.

> Quagmire, swampland, morass:
> The slime kingdoms,
> Domains of the cold-blooded,
> Of mud pads and dirtied eggs.

'It is as if I am betrothed to them', he wrote of the boglands near Mossbawn, where he spent his childhood. 'And I believe my betrothal happened one summer evening, thirty years ago, when another boy and myself stripped to the whit and bathed in a moss-hole, treading in the liver-thick mud, unsettling a smoky muck off the bottom and coming out smeared and weedy and darkened. We dressed again and went home in our wet clothes ... somehow initiated' (*Preoccupations*, 1980).

'The essence of Orkney's magic is silence, loneliness and the deep marvellous rhythms of sea and land, darkness and light,' wrote George Mackay Brown (1921–96), a poet and novelist who was rooted almost all his life in the Orkneys. 'Rackwick:

A Child's Scrapbook' (1989) recreates the past and present of one of his best-loved places in a deceptively simple collage of images.

> The valley was a green jar,
> corn crammed
> The green bowl
> brimmed with milk, honey, fish-oil
> Once, the green jar
> tilted at sixteen hungry doors
> Sealed in the jar now
> Dust of old laughter and grief
> They say, the jar flawed
> With heaviness of coins
> Long fallen, the jar – shards
> Half hidden in rushes
> Hills tell old stories. Cliffs
> Are poets with harps
> Brightness broached –
> Shoal, peatbog, sheaves
> Waver west, fish, with moon and stars.
> The sun's a cornstalk.

In *The Wild Places* (2007) Robert MacFarlane (b.1976) shows how deeply our literary heritage has affected the way in which we see wild places today. As he rambles, swims, climbs and gropes through forests, he is constantly reminded of books and myths about wild places. He celebrates wildness in history (the monks of Skellig, the ancient deepwood), in literature (Malory's 'Forest Sauvage', the Irish saga *Sweeney Astray*, B.B.'s *Brendon Chase*, in which two boys 'go feral', living wild in the forest instead of going back to boarding school, the wolves that pursue Kay Harker in John Masefield's *The Box of Delights*) and in myth. Wotan's Wild Hunt is echoed by a record in the *Anglo-Saxon Chronicle* of a 'furious host' rushing through the 'mirk', from Stamford to the coast in 1127, and legend has it that to this day King Arthur and his knights clatter along the hollow ways between Cadbury and Glastonbury.

Most moving of all is an anecdote in which the recollection of wild places puts into remission, at least temporarily, the war-induced insanity of Ivor Gurney, whose war poems often referred nostalgically to his native Gloucestershire. Helen Thomas, widow of the poet Edward, visited him in Dartford Mental Asylum in 1932. With her she took a map of Gloucestershire, hoping that it would remind Gurney of the walks he once took with Edward. 'He spent that hour revisiting his beloved home … spotting … a track, a hill, or a wood, and seeing it all in his mind's eye.'

WATERLANDS

The history and literature of our island country are intimately connected to water. Britain's conquerors were by necessity seafarers, and had to remain seafarers in order to extend the wealth of the realm. Our rivers, 'the bloodstream of the nation', were for centuries the lifeblood of commerce. They, not roads, dominated such early maps as the Bodleian Library's fourteenth-century Gough map of Britain, and the canal network that linked towns and rivers was an essential part of the industrial revolution. As prosperity increased, both the seaside and inland waters became magnets for holidaymakers, dinghy-sailors, fishermen and those just seeking to contemplate the many moods of this aspect of nature.

96

A CALM.

Writers have drawn upon waterscapes of all kinds to describe unforgettable adventures in childhood, romantic interludes in adulthood, nostalgic memories in old age and intimations of mortality.

Seaside holidays became increasingly popular in the nineteenth century, in part because sea air was felt to be a healthy antidote to the polluted atmosphere of towns and cities, in part because railways made the coast much more accessible. Seen from the snug interiors of the solidly built seaside villas of Regency times, storms could be admired as splendid spectacles. On balmier days promenades were made along the pier and dips into the sea modestly taken from bathing-machines. Lewis Carroll, author of *Alice in Wonderland* (1865) and *Alice Through the Looking-Glass* (1871), was in reality the Oxford don Charles Dodgson (1832–98). He grew up in the popular Yorkshire seaside resort of Whitby, but his 'Sea Dirge' reveals that he actually loathed the seashore, with its armies of nursery-maids belabouring children with wooden spades. Carroll's gently satiric poems, 'The Walrus and the Carpenter', 'The Lobster Quadrille' and 'The Mock Turtle's Story', all take place on beaches, mocking both the formality of the Victorian promenaders and such tediously educative books on seaside flora and fauna as Mrs Gatty's *Parables from Nature*.

Writers quickly saw the literary potential of the seaside holiday. Jane Austen's final novel *Sanditon* (1817), written in the last year of her life, was inspired by her visit to Worthing in 1805, and its plot revolves around the exaggeration of the place's development: both the number of visitors to the town and its size and elegance are greatly magnified by gossip.

> Everybody has heard of Sanditon – the favourite – for a young and rising bathing-place, certainly the favourite spot of all that are to be found along the coast of Sussex; the most favoured by nature and the most chosen by man.

When Charlotte Heywood and her family finally arrive at Sanditon, they find it empty of fashionable visitors and very unfinished. Mr Heywood's cynicism in the book's opening pages is more than justified. 'Every five years, one hears of some new place or other, starting up by the sea, and growing the fashion. How they can half of them be filled, is the wonder! Where can people be found with money and time to go to them! – Bad things for a country; sure to raise the price of provisions and make the poor good for nothing.' The genial Mr Parker delivers the book's moral: 'Those who tell their own story must be listened to with caution'. Ironically, the novel was in the end as unfinished as Sanditon itself.

The seaside was often presented as a place removed from normal conventions, one where transgressions can take place. In Jane Austen's *Persuasion* (1816), the headstrong and flirtatious Louisa Musgrove falls from the wave-lashed Cobb of Lyme Regis, precipitating a chain of events that will change her life. A century and a half later, in a teasing homage, John Fowles made Lyme Regis the setting for his novel *The French Lieutenant's Woman* (1969). Sarah Woodruff, suspected by the townspeople of being a fallen woman abandoned by her lover, spends long days gazing out to sea from the Cobb; she too sustains an ankle injury that will lead her deeper into social exclusion. Fowles also has in mind Thomas Hardy's seaside scenes in *Tess of the D'Urbervilles* (1891), in which Sandbourne (transparently Bournemouth) is endowed with glittery and ominous artificiality. When Angel Clare arrives there in search of Tess, who has been persuaded to go there with Alec D'Urberville, he sees it as

> a fairy place, suddenly created by the stroke of a wand, and allowed to get a little dusty. An outlying tract of the enormous Egdon Heath was close at hand, yet on the very verge of that tawny piece of antiquity such a glittering novelty as this pleasure city had chosen to spring up ... It was a city of detached mansions, a Mediterranean lounging-place on the English Channel.

The detached mansions are in fact stylish lodging houses, and in one of them Angel eventually finds Tess, tricked out in the fine clothes that her seducer has given her, but already hating him. The two of them stand transfixed, 'their baffled hearts looking out of their eyes with a joylessness pitiful to see. Both seemed to implore something to shelter them from reality'. Angel has the sense that 'his original Tess

PUNCH, OR THE LONDON CHARIVARI.—October 15, 1892.

"CROSSING THE BAR."

"TWILIGHT AND EVENING BELL,
AND AFTER THAT THE DARK!" | "AND MAY THERE BE NO SADNESS OF FAREWELL,
WHEN I EMBARK."—Tennyson.

had spiritually ceased to recognise the body before him as hers – allowing it to drift, like a corpse in the current, in a direction dissociated from its living will.'

Alfred, Lord Tennyson (1809–92) loved the seaside from childhood, when his holidays were spent at the east-coast resorts of Mablethorpe and Skegness in Lincolnshire. Coastal regions still fascinated the poet as an adult, and once the railway train could whirl him down to Bude, he toured the West Country in search of inspiration for the settings of his great Arthurian epic *Idylls of the King*. The eccentric but scholarly vicar of Morwenstow Robert Harker showed Tennyson around Tintagel and the black and ragged ledges of the North Devon shore, and lent him obscure legends. Tennyson's poetry was to make Tintagel and 'the thundering shores of Bude and Bos' as popular a tourist destination as Sir Walter Scott's novels did Loch Katrine and the Trossachs. After Tennyson succeeded Wordsworth as poet laureate and could afford to settle in style, he chose the Isle of Wight, moving into Farringford House. This substantial Georgian mansion, prettily gothicised with parapets and mullioned casement windows in 1810, was only a few minutes' walk from the white cliffs and curving strand of Freshwater Bay.

A powerful and enduring influence on Tennyson's work, the sea is linked with death in two of his best-known poems. After the death of his sister's fiancé and his own beloved friend Arthur Hallam, he composed the haunting lines:

> Break, break, break
> On the cold gray stones, O Sea –
> And I would that my tongue could utter
> The thoughts that arise in me ...
> Break, break, break
> At the foot of thy crags, O Sea!
> But the tender grace of a day that is dead
> Will never come back to me.

At the age of 80 Tennyson wrote 'Crossing the Bar', jotting down its 16 lines on the back of an envelope as he was crossing the Solent from Yarmouth to Lymington. He later requested that it always be printed as the last poem in any collection of his poetry. Set to music by Sir Frederick Bridge, it was sung at his funeral three years later.

LEFT
The Yarmouth scenes in Charles Dickens' *David Copperfield* were inspired by his own childhood holidays there. Fred Barnard's illustration of David's first sight of the Peggoty family's beached houseboat appeared in Chapman and Hall's handsome Household Edition of the book, published in 1872.

Both Sigmund Freud and Virginia Woolf regarded *David Copperfield* (1850) as Charles Dickens' masterpiece, and the author himself said it was his favourite book. Dickens' own seaside holiday in Great Yarmouth inspired the Norfolk settings of *David Copperfield*, especially the scenes in which David stays in Yarmouth in the Peggotty family's beached houseboat, 'picking up shells and pebbles' on the beach with the pretty and pragmatic Little Em'ly and 'stopping under the lee of the lobster-outhouse to exchange an innocent kiss'. Em'ly runs perilously far out on a high breakwater, a foreshadowing of her later seduction by Steerforth, whom David, oblivious of his true nature, will introduce like a serpent into her marine paradise.

Bram Stoker's *Dracula* (1897) introduces even more menace at the seaside. It is August, and the streets are bustling with trippers when a storm-blown Russian schooner labours into the harbour of Whitby, a pleasant Yorkshire seaside town. The ship's dead captain is lashed to its mast, and it will emerge that the great black dog that leaps ashore from the ship and disappears among the tombstones of the cliff-edge graveyard is the vampire Count Dracula himself. Stoker took his family on a holiday to the town in 1890, and was much taken by the looming ruins of Whitby Abbey and the atmospheric, bat-haunted graveyards. He sets the dramatic scene in which Mina witnesses without understanding Dracula's lethal embracing of Lucy on the East Cliff, high above the sea.

'At the edge of the West Cliff above the pier I looked across the harbour to the East Cliff, in the hope or fear, I don't know which, of seeing Lucy in our favourite seat. There was a bright full moon, with heavy, black, driving clouds, which threw the whole scene into a fleeting diorama of light and shade as they sailed across. For a moment or two I could see nothing, as the shadow of a cloud obscured St Mary's Church and all around it. Then, as the cloud passed, I could see the ruins of the Abbey coming into view, and as the edge of a narrow band of light as sharp as a sword-cut moved along, the church and the churchyard became gradually visible. Whatever my expectation was, it was not disappointed, for there, on our favourite seat, the silver light of the moon struck a half-reclining figure, snowy-white. The coming of the cloud was too quick for me to see much, for the shadow shut down on light almost immediately; but it seemed to me as though something dark stood behind the seat where the white figure shone, and bent over it. What it was, whether man or beast, I could not tell.'

Today Whitby uses the connection as a tourist attraction, offering tours along the cliffs in Dracula's footsteps and mounting an annual Goth Festival.

Best known for his searing First World War play *Journey's End* (1928), R.C. Sherriff (1896–1975) grew up in Hampton Wick, Middlesex, and was severely wounded at Passchendaele. He was a writer with the knack of making his readers sympathise fondly with characters who are both intensely ordinary and yet also universal. *The Fortnight in September* (1931) is the simplest of stories: it recounts every tiny detail of a seaside holiday loved because of its predictability from the ritual repetition of preparing the house to be left and the getting of tickets and places in the train to the noting of familiar landmarks and the intoxication of the actual arrival at Bognor.

> Here was the shop with the glistening wet fish, sleeping among its soft bed of freshly gathered seaweed – and the toy shop filled with spades and buckets, shrimping nets and yachts – with sheets of transfers and indoor games to play in the evenings when your legs are too tired to move, and your mind is peaceful and drowsy from its drenching with fresh air; and your face burns, although your eyes are cool.

As the days pass, we learn all about the hopes and fears of the Stevens family (father, mother, teenagers Mary and Dick and little Ernie); aspects of their characters kept well-hidden at home emerge as each rises to the challenges of being away. It might seem a surprising novel to write soon after *Journey's End*, but it was to just such mundane normalities that those who fought in the war longed to return.

Philip Larkin (1922–85) captured exactly the same reassuring ordinariness in his poem 'To the Sea' (*High Windows*, 1974). It was written after a visit to Southwold reminded him of childhood holidays, and

> The miniature gaiety of seasides.
> Everything crowds under the low horizon:
> Steep beach, blue water, towels, red bathing caps,
> The small hushed waves' repeated collapse
> Up the warm yellow sand, and further off
> A white steamer stuck in the afternoon.

Once Jung had identified the sea as a symbol of the collective unconsciousness, and Freud had declared childhood experience a profound influence on psychological development, many novels about the seaside were heavily freighted with symbolism. L.P. Hartley (1895–1972) set *The Shrimp and the Anemone* (1944) at Hunstanton, where he spent childhood holidays. Told from the point of view of nine-year-old Eustace, the novel opens as he is watching an anemone devour a shrimp in a rock pool, and

RIGHT
Richard Attenborough
as psychopathic Pinkie
and Carol Marsh as
trusting Rose in John
Boulton's 1947 film
of Graham Greene's
dark subversion of
the seaside idyll,
Brighton Rock.

wondering whether the shrimp deserves to be saved more than the anemone deserves
its food. Full of the same evocative holiday details as *Fortnight in September*, the book's
deeper purpose, developed in two sequels, is much darker: the shrimp, it will
emerge, is Eustace, the anemone his older sister Hilda. Already in his mind 'more
interesting and rarer' than he is, she will victimise him in later life. *The Shrimp and
the Anemone* closes with Hilda and Eustace running three-legged, Hilda's iron spade
'making jabs at the vitals of the future, while the wooden one that served Eustace as
a symbol of Adam's destiny [dangles] from his nerveless fingers.'

In 1938 another subversion of the seaside idyll was published. Graham Greene's
thriller *Brighton Rock* gives a dark modernist twist to the Prince Regent's favourite
watering-place. Scenes are set in Brighton's pubs and promenades, station tearooms and
tenements backing on the railway lines, and storms rolling in from the sea highlight
the tightening menace of the action. Mingling with the throngs of promenading
day-trippers eager for fun and amorous adventure are men with murder in mind.
Squalor and evil dwell in the smelly, asphalt basement yards that nestle beneath the
handsome Georgian bow windows of the holiday lodging houses, and in the 'dark
poison-bottle green' timbers under the glittering, silver-painted piers.

Seventeen-year-old Pinkie Brown is a cold-eyed sociopath. His head sings lines from Catholic liturgy as he murders Charlie Hale, an informer who betrayed the previous leader of his gang of racecourse touts. He subsequently sets out to seduce and marry Rose, a waitress who may have witnessed his clumsy attempt to create an alibi, so that she won't be able to testify against him. The steadiest character in the book is the blowsy and often inebriated Ida Arnold, motherly and forgiving, but 'a stickler where right's concerned'.

Pinkie, unforgettably played by Richard Attenborough in the 1947 film of the book, is drawn as irreversibly evil, his Roman Catholic upbringing no match for the psychopathic tendencies created by his loveless childhood. 'Tenderness stirred, but he was bound in a habit of hate.' Ida quickly realises how dangerous a husband he is for the gullible and innocent Rose, and tries to persuade her to leave him. Rose, heartbreakingly loyal, pleads that he may change; Ida warns her that he won't.

'It's like one of those sticks of rock: bite it all the way down, you'll still read Brighton.'
'Confession ... Repentance,' Rose whispered.
'That's just religion,' [Ida] said. 'Believe me, it's the world we got to deal with.'

In the final rain-drenched drive to the half-built edges of Peacehaven, where Pinkie plans to persuade Rose to shoot herself, their nightmare journey in the dark is repeatedly contrasted with the everyday: brightly lit buses; drinkers in the bar; and, oddest of all, the stained-glass bungalow window showing Frans Hals's *Laughing Cavalier* among roses that illuminates Rose as she tremblingly lifts the gun to her head.

Water and Memory

Where are your monuments, your battles, martyrs?
Where is your tribal memory? Sirs,
In that gray vault. The sea. The sea
Has locked them up. The sea is History.

Derek Walcott's poem 'The Sea is History' (1980) spells out the way in which the sea furnishes our memories; it also haunts and inspires them. One of the oldest examples of this is the Anglo-Saxon poem *The Seafarer*, which is told in the voice of an old sailor reminiscing about his years in the dragon boats. The first 30 lines describe the desolate hardships of life at sea in winter – the anxieties, icy wetness and solitude – in contrast to life on land where men are surrounded by kinsmen, free from dangers and full of food and wine. Then, as the climate on land begins to resemble that of the wintry sea, the speaker changes his tone and expresses his yearning for the sea in summer.

The cry of the gannet is all my gladness,
The call of the curlew, not the laughter of men,
The mewing gull, not the sweetness of mead ...
The groves burst with blossoms, towns become fair,
Meadows are beautiful once more, the whole world revives;
All these things urge the eager man
To set out on a journey over the salt streams.
(trans: Kevin Crossley-Holland)

The poet John Masefield (1878–1967) went to sea as a young man and suffered many hardships, but memories of those years infuse many of his novels and poems. In 'Sea-Fever' he longs for 'the gull's way, the whales' way'. Rudyard Kipling's poem 'The Sea and the Hills' (1902) expresses the same lyrical nostalgia:

Who hath desired the Sea? – the sight of salt water unbounded
The heave and the halt and the hurl and the rash of the comber wind-hounded?
The sleek-barrelled swell before storm, grey, foamless, enormous and growing –
Stark calm on the lap of the Line or the crazy-eyed hurricane blowing.

Matthew Arnold's bleakly nihilistic 'Dover Beach', sketched out at a time when the receding 'sea of faith' was disturbing many, and the prospect of war with Russia in the Crimea loomed, raises more profound issues. It begins by bidding the poet's companion to admire the moonlit night, then likens the 'tremulous cadence' of the waves on the pebbles to an 'eternal note of sadness'. Arnold made notes towards the poem in 1851, while waiting to cross from Dover to Calais on honeymoon, and it can be read as a plea to his bride:

> Ah love, let us be true
> To one another! For the wide world which seems
> To lie before us like a land of dreams
> So various, so beautiful, so new,
> Hath really neither joy, nor love, nor light,
> Nor certitude, nor peace, nor help for pain;
> And we are here as on a darkling plain
> Swept with confused alarms of struggle and flight,
> Where ignorant armies clash by night.

Hardly suitable as a bridal gift! Arnold wisely reserved the work; it was first published in 1867 and has remained such a perennial favourite that in 2005 it was cheerfully parodied by Daljet Nagra's poem 'Look we have coming to Dover'; no nihilism here, just the hopeful longing of immigrants 'hutched in a Bedford van' for 'a passport to life'.

Virginia Woolf (1882–1941) never forgot the seaside holidays which the family took in Talland House, St Ives, until the death of her mother in 1895. Although *To The Lighthouse* (1927) is set in the Hebrides, its descriptions are transparently of St Ives Bay.

> The great plateful of blue water was before her; the hoary Lighthouse, distant, austere, in the midst; and on the right, as far as the eye could see, fading and falling, in soft low pleats, the green sand dunes with the wild flowing grasses on them, which always seemed to be running away to some moon country, uninhabited of men.

One of the novel's several themes is how we perceive those around us, and Woolf seeks to unearth from her own fragmented memories the truth about her lost mother's reality. In this she succeeded so well that her sister Vanessa observed that reading descriptions of Mrs Ramsay was like seeing her mother raised from the dead. The sea is a constant presence, almost like a Greek chorus; when she was working on the book, Woolf wrote 'I am making up "To The Lighthouse" – the sea is to be heard all through it'.

106

RIGHT
Virginia Woolf,
To the Lighthouse.
Front cover of the
Hogarth Press edition
of 1927, designed by
Vanessa Bell.

OPPOSITE
The experience of
gazing hopefully over
to Godrevy Lighthouse,
the 'hoary Lighthouse,
distant, austere', from
St Ives was an annual
experience for Virginia
Woolf during her
childhood. Although
set in Scotland, her
novel *To the Lighthouse*
was a recreation of
the family's Cornish
holidays and a subtle
portrait of her mother.

[top left margin note:]
3/ Needs thinning + considering to avoid
repetitions & complexity - the [dramatic] elements
need classifying - ? [ ]

[top right margin note:]
which [ ] and [ ]
continents; which demolish
as it builds; which [ ]
simultaneous accretion [ ]
which is neither [ ] nor
decay.

// About the Fens
??? (and about silt)

[left margin notes, illegible:]
① [ ]
② [ ]
childism
[ ]

Which are a low-lying region of eastern England, over 1,200
square miles in area, bounded in the North and West by
the limestone hills of the Midlands and to the South and East
by the chalk hills of Cambridgeshire, Suffolk and Norfolk. To the
North the Fens advance, on a twelve mile front, to meet the North
Sea at the [ ], or perhaps it is [ ] to say that the Sea
[ ] the North sea in a perpetual bid to recapture [ ]
(its) former territory. For the chief fact about the Fens is that they
are reclaimed land, land that once was [ ], and even [ ]
the (new) dry land of the Fens still [ ] by [ ] to its
former state.

Once the shallow, feeble waters of the North [ ] and [ ]
of Boston and King's Lynn, but licked southwards as far as
Cambridge and Bedford. What caused them to [ ]? The answer
can be given in one word: silt. The Fens were formed by silt.
A word which when you utter it (letting the air [ ] between
your teeth), becomes a slow, tedious and insinuating [ ] accretion.
Silt: a word which (are you listening, S?) [ ] and disturbs
history. For long before the Egyptians built the pyramids or the
Greeks [ ] the Persians at [ ], silt was imperceptibly
changing the shape of coastlines and [ ] of rivers and
[ ] [ ] where no land was before. And what is all the
[ ] play-acting of history compared to the slow, muddy reality
of silt, to the silent [ ] and [ ] of [ ]
after particle, by which continents are remodelled? Silt which
demolishes as it builds; which is neither progress nor decay; which
[ ] simultaneous erosion and accumulation. A sobering
[ ] (for any man), but one which - since the house in
which he has long housed its solid foundations to silt - occupies a
special place in your history-mad [ ] mental catalogue(s). Which

Daphne du Maurier (1907–89) had a lifelong attachment to Cornish waters, forged by childhood holidays spent in Fowey. As soon as she could she settled there, and remained for the rest of her life. 'I walked this land with a dreamer's freedom and with a waking man's perception', she writes in the foreword to *Enchanted Cornwall* (1989). 'Places, houses, whispered to me their secrets and shared with me their sorrows and their joys. And in return I gave them something of myself, a few of my novels passing into the folk-lore of this ancient place.' *The House on the Strand* (1969), *Frenchman's Creek* (1941) and most of all *Rebecca* (1938) are works of high romance, inseparably linked to place and the past. The setting of Manderley, the house at the heart of *Rebecca*, was modelled on that of Menabilly, a house she first came across shuttered and closed-up – as Manderley would become at the end of *Rebecca*. 'The house possessed me from that day, even as a woman holds her lover', she later wrote in a memoir which described how she half-bullied it away from its owners. She wrote *Rebecca* when she was away from it – just as the book's heroine is in its first and last chapters

The fictional Manderley was much grander than Menabilly, but the beach-house, setting of the novel's most dramatic scenes and tragic climax, is a real building and still there, close by the Cornish Coast path. Here it was that the pretty little yacht *Je Reviens* became Rebecca's doom. Eventually the sea surrenders its secrets: the boat is hoisted out of the water and Rebecca's body is found inside. Although Max de Winter's crime escapes official detection, he is forced to tell the truth about the past to his second wife.

In the latter half of the twentieth century, the sea is seen more often than ever as a symbolic repository of memory. Both Iris Murdoch's *The Sea, The Sea* (1978) and John Banville's *The Sea* (2005) cast back to the protagonists' past. Graham Swift's *Waterland* (1983) is threaded through with history, this time of the East Anglian Fen Country, 'a landscape which, of all landscapes, most approximates to Nothing'. After a middle-aged history teacher loses his job because his wife steals a baby, he takes the reader back in time to his fenside youth, and the tragic death of a rival suitor for his wife's hand. The haunting atmosphere of the fenlands ('realism; fatalism; phlegm') counterpoints the human tragedies played out against its soft-edged, indefinite backdrop; its winding, semi-tidal waters resemble the way history works: 'It goes in two directions at once. It goes backwards as it goes forwards. It loops. It takes detours.'

Ian McEwan's *On Chesil Beach* (2007) is set in the 1960s (the time of McEwan's own youth). On a stony sterile strand, deliberately reminiscent of Arnold's 'Dover Beach', is played out the death of a relationship between two newly-weds too inhibited and embarrassed to survive a botched attempt at sex the night before. They part in 'grey, soft light and a delicate mist drifting in from the sea, whose steady motion of advance and withdrawal made sounds of gentle thunder, then suddenly hissing against the pebbles'. The novel delves back into each of the couple's pasts to reveal why they will never be able to be 'true to one another'.

Mystical Deep Streams

Isis and Osiris, the rivers of Alph and Lethe: myths of water as both border and passageway between life and death are commonplaces of ancient civilisations. Water has long been invested with magical power, and the Christian ritual of new life via baptism derives from John the Baptist's immersion of his converts in the River Jordan. No English book identified the soul's journey with water more literally than *The Water Babies* (1863), Charles Kingsley's morality tale for children. Written for his own children, it charts a symbolic evolutionary journey reflecting the fact that Kingsley (1819–75) had just read and marvelled at Charles Darwin's *On the Origin of Species* (1859). Ten-year-old Tom is a cruelly oppressed but indomitable little chimney sweep who gets lost in a maze of flues in the great house of Harthover and emerges into the virginally clean bedroom of little Miss Ellie. Accused of theft he panics, climbs out of the window and escapes across a moor that is distinctly Devonian, for all the book's official North Country setting and its collieries; there were in fact some small working coal mines in Devon at this time.

> Behind him, far below, was Harthover, and the dark woods, and the shining salmon river, and on his left, far below, was the town, and the smoking chimneys of the collieries; and far, far away, the river widened to the shining sea, and little white specks, which were ships, lay on its bosom ... A deep, deep green and rocky valley, very narrow, and filled with wood; but through the wood, hundreds of feet below him, he could see a clear stream glance. Oh, if he could but get down to that stream.

After many narrow escapes, and helped by an ageless Irish woman who reappears, like one of the Fates, in a variety of guises when he most needs her, Tom reaches his stream, 'a real North Country limestone fountain, like one of those in Sicily and Greece, where the old heathen fancied the nymphs sat cooling themselves the hot summer's day'. Stripping off his clothes, he slips into the water and is transformed into a four-inch-long, gill-frilled water-baby. Kingsley quotes Wordsworth's well-known line 'Our birth is but a sleep and a forgetting' at this point, to emphasise his

OPPOSITE
Mrs Bedonebyasyoudid gives Tom a pebble instead of a sweet as a punishment for putting stones in the mouths of sea anemones: Illustration by Jessie Wilcox Smith for a 1919 edition of *The Water Babies*, Charles Kingsley's tale of a soul's journey to salvation.

110

message that 'your soul makes your body, just as a snail makes his shell'. Tom is just as mischievous and naughty below the water as he was above it. He has to learn many hard lessons before he is shriven of sin and can be reborn into the world – and in the process child readers learn much about aquatic life. At the book's excessively fanciful end Tom meets Miss Ellie again and marries her; we leave him as 'a great man of science' who can 'plan railroads, and steam-engines, and electric telegraphs, and rifled guns, and so forth'.

Kingsley also employed landscape for effect in many of his rousingly patriotic stories. *Westward Ho!* (1855), a thrilling tale of Elizabethan privateers, begins and ends in Clovelly, North Devon, where he lived when young. The book became so popular that its name was given to the seaside resort that grew up nearby. In 1860 Kingsley, then Rector of Eversley in Hampshire, became Regius Professor of Modern History at Cambridge, after which he wrote his fenland historical romance *Hereward the Wake* (1865). Kingsley's interests were broad and another of his works, *Glaucus: Or the Wonders of the Shore* (1855), was written to encourage urban holidaymakers to teach their children to study marine ecology.

Happy, truly, is the naturalist. He has no time for melancholy dreams. The earth becomes to him transparent; everywhere he sees significance, harmonies, laws, chains of cause and effect endlessly linked, which draw him out of the narrow sphere of self-interest and self-pleasing, into a pure and wholesome region of solemn joy and wonder.

George Eliot's *The Mill on the Floss* (1860) tells the story of Tom and Maggie Tulliver, a fond brother and sister. Separated by Tom's anger at Maggie's involvement with men he deems unsuitable, they are eventually united by death, drowning together in the great flooding of the two rivers that join at their family's mill. Imagery of water made animate and potent suffuses the novel from beginning to end. 'The two bodies were found in close embrace', we are told on the book's last page, while its first page presages that tragedy: 'A wide plain, where the broadening Floss hurries on between its green banks to the sea, and the loving tide, rushing to meet it, checks its passage with impetuous embrace'.

Charles Dickens makes rivers the vehicles of fate in many of his novels. *Our Mutual Friend* (1865) opens with Gaffer Hexham, 'like a roused bird of prey', finding the body of what he hopes is a drowned man floating in the Thames. The lawyers sent to identify the body drive to Rotherhithe; 'down by where the accumulated scum of humanity seemed to be washed from higher grounds, like so much moral sewage, and to be pausing until its own weight forced it over the bank and sunk it in the river'. Further upstream, the river is used to symbolise renewed life; the decadent Eugene Wrayburn is saved from drowning and sees the error of his ways. In *Dombey and Son* (1848) the Thames is again likened to 'a stream of life'. Hurrying along London's crowded streets, Florence is

> Carried onwards into a stream of life ... flowing indifferently past marts and mansions, prisons, churches, market places, wealthy, poverty, good and evil, like the broad river side by side with it, awakened from its dream of rushes, willows, and green moss, and rolling on, turbid and troubled, among the works and cares of men, to the deep sea.

The sea, the end of the river's journey and by extension our own, is given a significant symbolic role in the novel. Little Paul Dombey, sent to Brighton for his health, is towed to the beach in a little cart. Here he sleeps for a while, then suddenly wakes and sits listening:

> Florence asked him what he thought he heard.
> 'I want to know what it says', he answered, looking her steadily in her face.
> 'The sea, Floy, what is it that it keeps on saying?'

She told him that it was only the noise of the rolling waves.

'Yes, yes,' he said. 'But I know that they are always saying something. Always the same thing. What place is over there?' He rose up, looking eagerly at the horizon.

She told him that there was another country opposite, but he said he didn't mean that; he meant farther away – farther away!

Very often afterwards, in the midst of their talk, he would break off, to try to understand what it was that the waves were always saying; and would rise up in his couch to look towards that invisible region, far away.

This passage inspired the hugely popular song 'What are the Wild Waves Saying, Sister', which goes further than Dickens did in spelling out that 'the voice of the great Creator/Dwells in that mighty tone'. Written by Joseph Carpenter, it was set to music by Stephen Glover and played on thousands of pianofortes as the reading public went into mourning after the much-loved character passed away. Dickens returns to Paul's question towards the end of the novel, when Florence has found happiness with Walter Gay. Together they watch the moonlit sea on their way to China, and remember Paul. Now it is made clear that the waves' song was the 'ceaseless murmuring of love – of love eternal and illimitable, not bounded by the confines of this world, or by the end of time, but ranging still, beyond the sea, beyond the sky, to the invisible country far away!' It is Old Dombey's failure to love except selfishly that causes his downfall as much as his pride.

Kenneth Grahame (1859–1932) brought pantheistic symbolism into *The Wind in the Willows* (1908), which is set on the Thames near Pangbourne, where he then lived. It portrays the river in varied seasonal moods, peopled with animals who are in part affectionate portraits of himself and his friends. Mole's penchant for domesticity and the Seafaring Rat's Cornish exploits were different facets of Grahame himself; the Water Rat's rivercraft and wanderlust belong to the energetic rowing antiquary F.J. Furnival, and the Cornish-based Seafaring Rat was Sir Arthur Quiller Couch. Toad's bombastic self-importance has been seen as a satirical reference both to the pleasure-loving Edward VII and to the flamboyant Oscar Wilde, who had been, as Toad becomes, a prisoner in Reading Gaol. Toad is also Grahame's way of criticising modern vulgarities such as motorcars and flashy clothes.

For Grahame, the book's most important chapter was 'The Piper at the Gates of Dawn', deliberately placed at its centre. In it the Rat and the Mole, searching as the dawn rises for a lost baby otter, find themselves drawn to an island by the sounds of pipes. 'O Mole!' sighs the Rat.

LEFT
'Splendid curves of shaggy limbs disposed in majestic ease': Kenneth Grahame placed Pan, 'the Friend and Helper', at the heart of his *The Wind in the Willows*: illustration by Arthur Rackham for the 1940 edition.

OPPOSITE
'Helper and healer I cheer small waifs in the woodland wet': Original 1908 manuscript showing the song of Pan that the Rat hears whispered by the reeds set out in verse form.

4

Lest the awe should dwell
And turn your frolic to fret
You shall look on me full my power at the helping hour
— But then you shall forget

Fear the helper Lest the limbs shall be reddened & rent
I spring the trap that is set
As I loose the snare (you may catch glimpse see me there
For yet surely you shall forget

Helper stealer I ~~took above~~ cheer
(Help stealing ~~song~~ cheer)
Small Earth waifs in the woodlands wet
With ~~Strays~~ Strays I find in it wounds I bind in it
Bidding them all forget

None shall hag for the pipers play
And none shall feel the debt
As I pipe your sadness into gladness

wet
debt
let
met
net
pet

'The beauty of it! The merry bubble and joy, the thin clear happy call of the
distant piping. Such music I never dreamed of, and the call in it is stronger
even than the music is sweet! Row on, Mole, row! For the music and the
call must be for us.'

The Mole, greatly wondering, obeyed. 'I hear nothing myself', he said, 'but
the wind playing in the reeds and rushes and osiers.'

The Rat never answered, if, indeed, he heard. Rapt, transported, trembling,
he was possessed in all his senses by this new, divine thing that caught up
his helpless soul and swung and dandled it, a powerless but happy infant in
a strong, sustaining grasp.

Suddenly they have an awe-inspiring vision of Pan, 'the Friend and Helper', with
gleaming horns, hooked nose, kindly eyes, rippling muscles and 'splendid curves of
shaggy limbs disposed in majestic ease'. The baby otter is sleeping peacefully on his lap.

Modern editors have sometimes omitted the whole chapter, underestimating a
child's hunger for wonder. But the book's original title was *The Wind in the Reeds*, and
Grahame, an admirer of Henry Thoreau's *Walden* (1854), intended the appearance of
Pan to be the climax of a book that was a call for his contemporaries to appreciate the
simple pleasures of the river rather than being distracted by the hectic pace of modern
life. The chapter title has since been borrowed by John Middleton Murray for a short
story, by Van Morrison for a song, and by Pink Floyd for their debut album.

Many poets have adopted rivers as their own. The seventeenth-century mystic
Henry Vaughan (1621–95) lived close to the river Usk, in the Welsh border country. In
his long poem 'To the river Isca', he imagined both classical Helicon and biblical Sion
in the hills around it, and prayed that its green banks and streams might stay 'fresh
as the air and clear as Glass', free from 'evet and toad' and 'wily winding snake'. He
found in its flowing waters a symbol of God's redemptive love: 'What sublime truths
and wholesome themes/Lodge in thy mystical, deep streams!'.

Wordsworth wrote a series of sonnets to the river Duddon, a Cumbrian stream
he had loved since his Cockermouth childhood. He traces it from its source high
on Wrynose Pass, from 'cradled Nursling of the mountain' to 'a glistering snake ...
thridding with sinuous lapse the rushes'. The 'undaunted Rill' grows into 'a Brook of
loud and stately march, crossed ever and anon by plank or arch'. Druids, Orinooko,
Danish Ravens and Roman eagles all feature; lovelorn maidens peep into 'Dian's
looking glass'; shepherds wash their flocks in its water. Finally his Sonnet 32 defined
the continuously renewed being of all rivers. 'Still glides the Stream, and shall for
ever glide;/The Form remains, the Function never dies.'

The poet Norman Nicholson (1914–87) lived all of his life at Millom, on the
Duddon Estuary, and the craggy skyline of the central Cumbrian fells, together with
the becks and rivers that flowed down from them, shaped his poetry. He loved the

Duddon just as Wordsworth had, and pictured the bard there in his own poem 'To the River Duddon' (1944).

> An oldish man with a nose like a pony's nose,
> Broad bones, legs long and lean but strong enough
> To carry him over Hard Knott at seventy years of age.
> He came to you first as a boy with a fishing rod
> And a hunk of Ann Tyson's bread and cheese in his pocket
> Walking from Hawkshead across Walna Scar ...

Nicholson was deeply religious. 'Part of the sheer enjoyment of being among mountains comes from our sometimes feeling swept up in the plan, where every end is a new beginning and every death a new birth'. Later in the poem he condemned Coleridge, 'the poet and heretic' to whom 'the fells were like a blackboard for the scrawls of God', and praised Wordsworth, 'the old man, inarticulate and humble', who 'Knew that eternity flows in a mountain beck'.

Henry Williamson (1895–1977) lived close to the Taw and the Torridge in North Devon. Both were immortalised in *Tarka the Otter: His Joyful Water-Life and Death in the Country of the Two Rivers* (1927). The poet Ted Hughes loved the same rivers with a fisherman's heart and a naturalist's eye, and also lived close to them for much of his life. One critic likened reading Hughes' light-hearted, country-wise collection *River* (1983) to 'immersing ourselves in *Field and Stream* while listening to Handel's *Water Music*'. It charts a year in the life of the river beginning on the morning before Christmas Eve, with poems full of images of the watery death and birth of salmon, eels and other water creatures, 'a solution of dead-ends – an all-out evacuation ... to the sea's big re-think', watched over with predatory intent by herons, owls and otters. Alternately lyrical and technical, symbolic and scientific, it is a treasure-box of fishing lore, water myths and pen portraits of particular rivers, charged with unexpected metaphors. 'A bluetit de-rusts its ratchet' and salmon 'toil, Trapped face-workers, in their holes of position, / Under the mountain of water'.

BELOW
Cover of the first edition of Henry Williamson's classic of nature observation, *Tarka the Otter* (1927), which was set in the 'Country of the Two Rivers', the Taw and the Torridge in North Devon 1927. Wood-engraving by Hester Sainsbury.

117

By Hester Sainsbury

Tarka the Otter

HIS JOYFUL WATER LIFE AND
DEATH IN THE COUNTRY OF
THE TWO RIVERS

By HENRY WILLIAMSON

ABOVE
'South-south-west and
down the contours.
I go slipping between
Black Ridge and White
Horse Hill into a bowl
of the moor where
echoes can't get
out'. Alice Oswald's
poem 'Dart' (2002)
weaves the river's past
and present into a
meandering whole.

In her 48-page poem 'Dart' (2002) Alice Oswald is figuratively, and occasionally literally, immersed in the river. She first discovers it as 'a trickle coming out of bark, a foal of a river' at Cranmere Pool, and finally watches its Protean transformation into the sea at Dartmouth, shepherding a school of seals. People's stories real and relayed punctuate the river's progress ('all voices should be read as the river's mutterings'). Brutus set sail for Troy from Dartmouth, river pilots complain of arthritis, millers wash their wool, sewage works dump shit. The river is sometimes wild, sometimes useful, sometimes treacherous, sometimes benign.

In recent times water has been worshipped with a new profundity by such writers as Roger Deakin (*Waterlog*, 1999) and Adam Nicolson (*Sea Room*, 2001). Fanciful symbolism is replaced by the awareness of how close we are to losing the natural beauties that we have taken for granted for too long.

Sweet Thames, Run Softly ...

Writers have been in love with the Thames for centuries, aware how richly English history flows in its current. The tireless antiquary John Leland (1503–52) published his 'Swan Song' (*Cygnea Cantio*) in 1545. In it a swan glides down the Thames from Oxford to Greenwich, noting such historical monuments as Runnymede and Windsor, and fulsomely singing the praise of his patron, Henry VIII. Both Edmund Spenser and the historian and poet William Camden (1551–1623) wrote poems on the marriage of the rivers Isis and Tame near Dorchester, thus, legend has it, creating the Thames. Spenser also apostrophised the Thames near the river Lee in *Prothalamion* (1596), his wedding song celebrating the marriage of the twin daughters of the Earl of Worcester, whom he likened to water nymphs; its much quoted refrain is 'Sweet Thames, run softly, till I end my song'.

Under the Stuart kings, the resourceful Thames waterman John Taylor (1578–1653), a brilliant self-publicist, styled himself 'the Kings Majesties Acqua-Muse'. Son of a Gloucester barber-surgeon, he became a Thames waterman, conscripted at the age of 18 to fight the Spanish as a seaman in the Earl of Essex's fleet. Returning to the Thames, he rose to become clerk of the London Guild of Watermen and organiser of pageants for special occasions. Watermen were the seventeenth-century equivalent of taxi-drivers, and every bit as prone to pontificating to their captive audiences. Taylor went on to publish over 150 poems, financed by subscription; he also attempted to cross the Thames in a boat made of hempseed paper using stockfish tied to bamboo canes as oars.

Other feats of the 'Gypsy Sculler' included rowing (in a rather more substantial boat) from London and the Thames round the coast to the Ouse and York, and venturing on excursions along the Severn, the Wye and the Hampshire Avon. Seeing the number of obstructions to navigation and the polluted nature of such waterways, he began a campaign to improve matters.

> I truly treat, that men may note and see
> What blessings navigable rivers are
> And how that thousands are debarred those blessings
> By few men's ambitious hard oppressings ...
> For as a monument to our disgraces
> The River's too too fowle in many places
> ('John Taylor's Last Voyage', 1641)

Charles I took him seriously, and Taylor accompanied a commission appointed to submit proposals on the dredging and purifying of the Thames. In 1632 he published his rhyming record of the commissioners' exploratory journey 'Taylor on Thame Isis ... With all the flats, shoares, shelves, sands, weares, stops, rivers, brooks, bournes,

THE
SCVLLER,

Rowing from TIBER to THAMES
with his Boate laden with a hotch-potch,
or Gallimawfry of Sonnets, Satyres,
and Epigrams.

With an addition of Pasto-
rall Equiuocques or the complaint
of a Shepheard.

By IOHN TAYLOR.

Sum primus homo, Vis ire mecum Remis? Eſt mihi proxima cimbe.

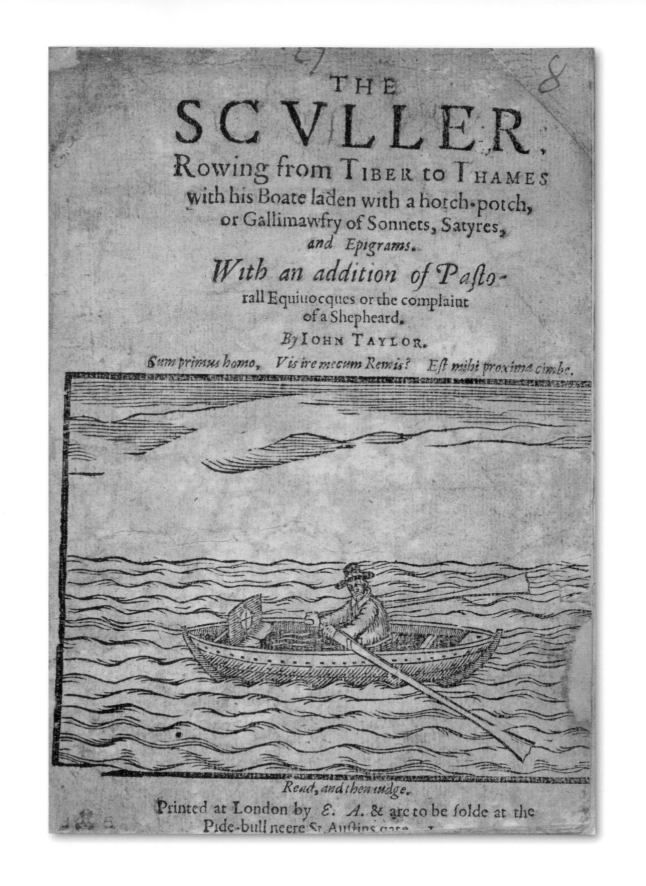

Read, and then iudge.

Printed at London by E. A. & are to be ſolde at the
Pide-bull neere St. Auſtins gate.

streams, rills, rivulets, streamlets, creeks, and whatsoever helps the said rivers have, from their springs or heads, to their falls into the ocean. As also a discovery of the hindrances which doe impeach the passage of boats and barges, betwixt the famous University of Oxford and the City of London' in 1632. Full of digressions and idiosyncratic opinion, and never letting accuracy get in the way of a good story, it makes excellent reading. As Taylor said himself,

> ...I have described the way we went,
> Commixing truth with honest merriment,
> My threadbare wit with a mad wool-gathering goes,
> To show the things in verse I saw in prose.

Thomas Gray, Thomas Love Peacock, Matthew Arnold and Oscar Wilde all wrote long poems about the Thames, while Lewis Carroll was inspired to make up the story of *Alice in Wonderland* during a rowing trip up to Godstow with the three daughters of the head of the college, Dean Liddell.

> All in the golden afternoon
> Full leisurely we glide;
> For both our oars, with little skill,
> By little arms are plied,
> While little hands make vain pretence
> Our wanderings to guide.
>
> Ah, cruel Three! In such an hour
> Beneath such dreamy weather,
> To beg a tale of breath too weak
> To stir the tiniest feather!
> Yet what can one poor voice avail
> Against three tongues together?
> Imperious Prima flashes forth
> Her edict 'To begin it'.
> In gentle tone Secunda hopes
> 'There will be nonsense in it!' –
> While Tertia interrupts the tale
> Not more than once a minute.

In *Alice Through the Looking Glass*, Carroll made another allusion to the Thames. In the chapter 'Wool and Water', Alice finds the White Queen has changed into a knitting sheep.

OPPOSITE
Title page of *The Sculler* (1612), a 'hotch-potch' of sonnets and satires by the Thames waterman John Taylor, who prided himself on being James I's 'Acqua-Poet'.

121

'Can you row?' the Sheep asked, handing her a pair of knitting needles as she spoke.

'Yes a little, but not on land – and not with needles –' Alice was beginning to say when suddenly the needles turned to oars in her hands, and she found they were in a little boat, gliding between the banks.

This was inspired by the dramatic Inundation of Christ Church Meadows, pictured in *The Illustrated London News* in 1852. It occurred during Carroll's second winter in Oxford, when rail travellers had to row to the station in boats and ground floor rooms in Christ Church were flooded.

The designer, artist and writer William Morris (1834–96) settled beside the upper reaches of the Thames at Kelmscott Manor. He filled the ancient house with beautifully handcrafted furniture, tapestries and books.

> What better place than this, then, could we find?
> By this sweet stream that knows not of the sea,
> That guesses not the city's misery,
> This little stream, whose hamlets scarce have names,
> This far-off, lonely mother of the Thames.
> (*Earthly Paradise: June*)

In the 1880s Londoners in search of pleasure ventured out in punts and skiffs on the Thames upstream of Teddington Lock, where the river ceased to be affected by the tide. Jerome K. Jerome (1859–1927) and his wife spent much of their honeymoon in a small boat on the Thames in 1888, and a year later Jerome published *Three Men in a Boat (to say nothing of the Dog)* – a comic travelogue about both the new fashion for boating and the sordid realities of a camping holiday on the river. Beginning at Kingston and heading towards Oxford, the journey was based on the boating trips he often took with two friends; the dog was, apparently, purely imaginary. Jerome's honeymoon may explain the occasional sentimental passages, but they may also be intended to poke fun at the much more usual literary convention of nature worship. In a half-teasing, half-serious passage, Jerome identifies the city-dwellers' growing alienation from nature:

We are creatures of the sun, we men and women. We love light and life. That is why we crowd into the towns and cities, and the country grows more and more deserted every year. In the sunlight – in the daytime, when Nature is alive and busy all around us, we like the open hillsides and the deep woods well enough: but in the night, when our Mother Earth has gone to sleep, and left us waking, oh! The world seems so lonesome, and we get frightened, like children in a silent house. Then we sit and sob, and long for the gas-lit streets,

and the sounds of human voices and the answering throb of human life. We feel so helpless and little in the great stillness, when the dark trees rustle in the night-wind. There are so many ghosts about, and their silent sighs make us feel so sad.

John Betjeman (1906–84) was undoubtedly a Thames-in-the-daytime man, who preferred to be tucked safely up under an eiderdown rather than shivering in a tent. In his poem 'Henley', he whimsically asks

ABOVE
'A party of provincial 'Arrys and 'Arriets out for a moonlight sail'. Illustration by A. Frederic for the first edition of Jerome K. Jerome's comic Thames travelogue *Three Men in a Boat* (1889).

> When shall I see the Thames again?
> The prow-promoted gems again,
> As beefy ATS
> Without their hats
> Come shooting through the bridge?
> And 'cheerioh' and 'cheeri-bye'
> Across the waste of waters die
> And low the lists of evening lie
> And lightly skims the midge.

More bleakly, T.S. Eliot parodied Spenser's famous lines.

> The river's tent is broken; the last fingers of leaf
> Clutch and sink into the wet bank. The wind
> Crosses the brown land, unheard. The nymphs are departed.
> Sweet Thames, run softly, till I end my song.
> The river bears no empty bottles, sandwich papers,
> Silk handkerchiefs, cardboard boxes, cigarette ends
> Or other testimony of summer nights. The nymphs are departed
> And their friends, the loitering heirs of city directors –
> Departed, have left no addresses.
> (*The Waste Land*, III Fire Sermon, 1922)

Robert Gibbings paid Spenser less ironic homage in the titles of his two books on the Thames, *Sweet Thames Run Softly* (1940) and *Till I End My Song* (1958). His approach to the river was a mixture of the historical commentary of Leland, the playful spirit of John Taylor and the earnest naturalist observations of C.J. Cornish, but he was also conscious of the impact on it of modern times.

> Talk about the sacred Ganges. It is nothing to the Thames at Chiswick. And there were children bathing, swimming in water the colour of beer, with a sediment on its surface thick enough to be the beginning of a new continent.

Once the Thames reaches London, its use as a muse increases exponentially. It is both highway and edge, escape route and threat to life. In medieval and Tudor times, when the Scottish poet William Dunbar could praise the river's 'beryl streams, pleasant and preclare ... where many a swan doth swim with wings fair', the palaces of the wealthy lined its northern bank, while Shakespeare's plays were acted out in the Globe Theatre on its more alternative Southwark shore. The river has been a magnet for London's men of letters: Samuel Pepys, busy with naval matters at Trinity House, was rowed up and down it; Dr Johnson lived close to it in Fleet Street; Wordsworth stood on Westminster Bridge and exclaimed that 'Earth had not anything to show more fair'. By then, however, the Thames was already becoming 'the Great Stink' of Victorian times, and it haunts the writings of Dickens like an omen. 'The river had an awful look, the buildings on the bank were muffled in black shrouds, and the reflected lights seemed to originate deep in the water, as if the spectres of suicides were holding them to show where they went down', he wrote in *The Uncommercial Traveller* (1860).

H.G. Wells ends his novel *Tono-Bungay* (1909) with a heavily symbolic journey down to the mouth of the Thames, freighted with comment on the ethics of Empire.

125

OPPOSITE
Robert Gibbings rowed down the Thames in a home-made skiff called Willow, enjoying the encounters with wild things and people on the way downstream: wood engraving from *Sweet Thames Run Softly* (1940).

Light after light goes down. England and the Kingdom, Britain and the Empire, the old prides and the old devotions, glide abeam, astern, sink down upon the horizon, pass – pass. The river passes – London passes, England passes.

Wells would have been familiar with Joseph Conrad's *Heart of Darkness* (1899), a novella which was, for its time, an unusual and radical indictment of white settlers' abuse of Africans. But Conrad's tale develops into a more general condemnation of the darkness that lurks beneath the surface of even the most civilised human beings. Kurtz, the ivory trader at the centre of the story, is a 'universal genius' who

becomes warped by fantasies of omnipotence and is eventually destroyed by what he has himself set in motion. The story of Kurtz is told aboard a sailing boat moored off Tilbury by Charlie Marlow, a trader who went up river and discovered Kurtz's terrible fate. Conrad uses the estuary scenes for symbolic premonition. Before Charlie begins his tale, the men on the boat watch the sun as it sinks into the black clouds looming over London, 'changed to a dull red without rays and without heat, as if about to go out suddenly, stricken to death by the touch of that gloom brooding over a crowd of men'.

Conrad had read William Booth's stirring indictment of the London slums,

In Darkest England and the Way Out (1890), and noted its deliberate parody of Henry Stanley's *In Darkest Africa*, which was published earlier in 1890. Conrad's narrator dwells complacently on the centuries of glorious maritime history evoked by the 'venerable stream bathed in the august light of abiding memories', but Marlow abruptly changes the mood, suddenly saying, 'And this also ... has been one of the dark places of the earth'. He goes on to explain that he was thinking of the coming of the Romans, 'the military camp lost in a wilderness – cold, fog, tempests, disease, exile, and death'.

> Or think of a decent young citizen in a toga – perhaps too much dice, you know – coming out here in the train of some prefect, or tax-gatherer, or trader even, to mend his fortunes, land in a swamp, march through the woods, and in some inland post feel the savagery, the utter savagery, had closed round him, – all that mysterious life of the wilderness that stirs in the forest, in the jungles, in the hearts of wild men.

So it is that the tale Marlow goes on to tell is made as true to England as it is of Africa. In the closing scene, the pall over London has spread to the east as well. 'The offing was barred by a black bank of clouds, and the tranquil waterway leading to the uttermost ends of the earth flowed sombre under an overcast sky – seemed to lead into the heart of an immense darkness.'

Iain Sinclair's *Downriver* (1991) is a series of extravagantly gothic and frequently surreal scenes that contrast London's West End with the Thames badlands; like *The Waste Land*, it is threaded with ironic literary references.

> Wooden stumps in the mud. The ruins of a jetty. The tide was turning: a slime-caked causeway, plastered in filth and sediment, pointed at Gravesend. [Bobby] often boasted, without much justification, that Magwitch faltered here, escaping from the hulks, and was brought to shore. The last pub in the world, the World's End.

Set in the last years of Margaret Thatcher's premiership, and fuelled by Sinclair's resentment at the gentrification of his native Hackney, the book is a frenetic satire on the obscene extremes of wealth and poverty – less a novel than poetry extended into prose. Sinclair mutates the ordinary with startlingly memorable images: 'Out on the river, eight giants – heads in laps – were tongue-lashed by a squeaking midget' is how he describes a rowing eight on the Thames in *Radon's Daughters* (1994).

There is a cinematic exactness in his descriptions, as if London's life, with all its irrelevant details, has been freeze-framed. *Downriver* is indeed loosely structured around 12 photographic postcards, supposedly found in a Tilbury junkshop and put in order by Sinclair's friend Joblard, who gives them the title *Heart of Darkness*. To Sinclair's mind, London's river has now become as savage and wild as Marlow had imagined it to have been in the time of the Romans.

> The river *is* time: breathless, cyclic, unstoppable. It offers immersion, blindness: a poultice of dark clay to seal our eyes forever from the fear and agony of life. Events, and the voices of events, slurp and slap, whisper their liquid lies: false histories in mud and sediment; passions reduced to silt.

Of the making of books inspired by the Thames there will be no end. One of the latest and most unusual is *Thames to Dunkirk* (2009), a 17m-long freestanding paper sculpture by Liz Matthew which is in the form of a monumental book. The text is a combination of typewritten lines from B.G. Bonallack's poem telling the story of the retreat from Dunkirk, and calligraphically inscribed lines from Virginia Woolf's *The Waves* which run underneath them; between the two, a wavering blue line represents first the estuary and then, as it widens into blue, the sea itself. The coast of Dunkirk appears, war-torn and smoking, and 'strong hands reached out' towards the soldiers in the water, each symbolised by a single letter.

129

Iain Sinclair

DOWNRIVER

'CRAZY, DANGEROUS, PROPHETIC'
ANGELA CARTER, *LONDON REVIEW OF BOOKS*

COCKNEY VISIONS

Eternal London

London has always fascinated and appalled writers in equal measure. In the latter part of the fourteenth century, William Langland bemoaned its seedier aspects in his *Vision of Piers Plowman*, and in the 1390s Geoffrey Chaucer, comfortably ensconced above Aldgate as Controller of Customs and court poet, devised his tales of pilgrims gathering in Southwark to set off for Canterbury. Even then it was a city disproportionate in size to any other place in Britain, and the literature it has generated is one of exaggeration and excess, of hyperbole and variety, frequently scatological, often theatrical, and with a strong vein of protest running through it.

132

ABOVE
Panorama of London of 1588 by William
Smith: even in Elizabethan times, London
was far larger than any other British city,
and it engendered a literature of excess.

CHAPTER OPENER
'Dark satanic mill?'
Thomas Rowlandson's
depiction of the
destruction in 1791 of
Albion Mills, which
once stood on the site
of the Royal Festival
Hall and may have
inspired William Blake.

BELOW
Geoffrey Chaucer lived
above Aldgate, and
references to London
run through his Tales.
He is portrayed holding
his famous book
in this illuminated
capital letter in an
early fifteenth-century
manuscript of *The
Canterbury Tales*.

'English drama, and the English novel, spring out of the very conditions of London', observes Peter Ackroyd in *London: The Biography* (2000). 'Nymphs have been seen along the banks of its rivers, and minotaurs within its labyrinths of brick. It has been aligned with Nineveh and Tyre, Sodom and Babylon, and at times of fire and plague the outlines of those cities have risen among its streets and buildings. The city's topography is a palimpsest within which all the most magnificent or monstrous cities of the world can be discerned. It has been the home of both angels and devils striving for mastery. It has been the seat of miracles, and the harbour of savage pessimism. Who can fathom the depths of London?'

Many long books have been dedicated to mapping London's literature. Here we concentrate on a handful of aspects: its ancient origins, its dark reputation among some writers as a 'city of dreadful night' and the love that it inspires in others, who point up its capacity for surviving against the odds, its nature as a vibrant cosmopolis capable of infinite renewal.

According to the *Brut*, a Middle English narrative poem recounting the 'history' of Britain, the land of Albion was discovered by the mythical Brutus, great-grandson of the Trojan hero Aeneas. Brutus defeated and killed the giants inhabiting Albion, renaming his domain Britain after himself. He established his capital on the banks of the Thames, calling it New Troy. In 1501 the Scottish poet William Dunbar recalled the legend in his poem 'To the City of London', apostrophising the capital as

Part of the earliest known version of William Langland's *Piers Plowman*, late fourteenth century.

> Flower of Cities all ... thou lusty Troynovaunt ...
> Gemme of all joy, jasper of jocundities,
> Most myghty carbuncle of vertue and valour;
> Strong Troy in vigour and in strenuytie.

Although William Langland's *Piers Plowman* famously opens with a vision, dreamt 'on a May morning on Malvern Hills', of a tower (heaven), a dungeon (hell) and 'a fair field full of folk', Langland's income derived from copying legal documents and singing masses for the souls of the dead. Southwark and Cock Lane, notorious haunts of whores, Cheapside, full of stalls of dubiously acquired merchandise, and Tyburn and its terrifying gallows all figure in his verse. His descriptions of the villainous hypocrites who crowd a London church, then adjourn to the inn, herald centuries of literary references to taverns, gin-shops and pubs.

> Hick the Hackneyman and Hugh the Needle,
> Clarice of Cock's Lane and the Clerk of the church,
> Sire Piers of Pridie, and Pernelle of Flanders,
> Davey the Diker, and a dozen others:
> A Ribibour, a Ratoner, a Rakiere of Cheap.

ABOVE
Part of the earliest known version of William Langland's *Piers Plowman*, late fourteenth century. Although the narrator falls asleep in the Malvern Hills, *Piers Plowman* contains many detailed topographical descriptions of London streets and life in the capital.

Whan that aprille with his sholres soote
The drought of marche hay perced to ye roote
And bathud euery veyne in swich licour
Of which vertue engendred is ye flour
Whan zephirus eek with his swete breeth
Enspired hath in euery holte and heeth
The tendre croppes and ye zonge sonne
Hath in ye ram his halfe cours ironne
And smale fowles maken melodie
That slepen al ye night wiy open yhe
So priketh hem nature in here corages
Thanne longen folk to gon on pilgrimages
And palmers for to seeken straunge strondes
To ferne halwes couthe in sondry londes
And specially from euery shires ende
Of Engelond to Canturbury yey wende
The holy blisful marty for to seeke
That hem hay holpen whan pat yey were seeke

Byfel pat in pat sesoun on a day
In Southwerk at ye Tabbard as I lay
Redy to wenden on my pilgrimage
To canturbury with ful deuout corage
At night was come in to pat hostelrie
Wel nyne and twenty in a companye
Of sondry folk by auenture I falle
In felaschipe and pilgryms were yai alle
That toward canturbury wolden ryde
The chambres and ye stables weren wyde
And wel we weren esid atte beste
And shortly whan ye sonne was to reste
So hadde I spoken with hem euerychon
That I was of here felaschipe anon
And made forward erly to aryse
To take oure weye ther as I zow deuyse
But natheles whiles I haue tyme and space

Langland describes how, in the tavern afterwards, Glutton 'glubs' a gallon and a gill of ale, and

> His guts began to growl as two angry sows;
> He pissed a pot in a Paternoster-while,
> And blew his round ruwet at his ruggebone's end,
> That all that heard that horn held their nose after.

Geoffrey Chaucer (c.1343–1400) was a cultured man of the world. He had fought in France, undertaken diplomatic missions for Richard II and served as both a judge and an MP. More sophisticated than Langland, he was also wittier and more scabrous. Although Chaucer's sources were French and Italian he wrote in English, then becoming the language of choice at court now that France was the national enemy. The English he wrote was recognisably that of his home patch. Chaucer was a Londoner to his backbone, lightning-fast and occasionally obscene in repartee. He revelled in theatrical artifices as he tucked tale within tale, concocting reasons to switch abruptly and dramatically from the high-minded Knight to the lascivious Miller, the genteel and hypocritical Prioress to the gloriously vulgar Wife of Bath. In later life he became more prosperous and moved out to London's salubrious Kent fringes, but he always kept his old eyrie above Aldgate, from which he could see the endless flow of London types passing by.

In his painting of 1808, 'Sir Jeffrey Chaucer and the Nine and Twenty Pilgrims on their journey to Canterbury', William Blake (1757–1827) drew the cast leaving the Tabard Inn in Borough High Street in a symbolically ordered procession, carefully varying the horses to suit their riders. Blake paid tribute to Chaucer as 'the great poetical observer of men', and his pilgrims as having 'the physiognomies or lineaments

137

of universal human life. As Newton numbered the stars, and as Linnaeus numbered the plants, so Chaucer numbered the classes of men'.

The pilgrims of *The Canterbury Tales* were largely Londoners. The Prioress hailed from Bow and the Sergeant of Law from the porch of St Paul's. The Merchant probably came from Lombard Street, the Manciple from the Inner Temple and the Pardoner from St Anthony's Hospital at Charing Cross. Meanwhile the Haberdasher, Carpenter, Weaver, Dyer and Maker of Tapestries (none of whose Tales Chaucer got round to writing) must all have been London guildsmen: they had hired a Cook, who 'knew all about London beer'. Most colourful of all was Harry Bailey, the genial Host of the Tabard Inn, a renowned server of good fish and flesh, washed down with strong and potable wine: 'You could not find a fairer citizen in the whole of Cheapside'. Only two of the Tales, the Canon's Yeoman's story of a greedy chantry priest duped by an alchemist, and The Cook's Tale, take place in the capital. Yet, although the rest range far and wide across geography, history and myth, the personalities of the characters in them struck chords with the listening Londoners.

London has been portrayed in literature as both a theatre and a prison, an earthly paradise and a halfway house to hell. It has always been a place of spectacle and performance. Medieval street pageants and travelling players were succeeded in

Tudor times by full-scale theatrical productions. Bartholomew Fair, first held in 1133 and the capital's longest-running piece of street theatre, was held in Smithfield, site of slaughterhouses and executions. Its pimps, whores and thieves peopled Ben Jonson's comedy *Bartholomew Fair*, first staged in 1614. In 1777, James Boswell recorded Dr Johnson's famous remark that 'when a man is tired of London, he is tired of life; for there is in London all that life can afford'. William Wordsworth looked at the scene from Westminster Bridge in 1802 and declared that 'Earth has not anything to show more fair', though he described Bartholomew Fair as a 'Parliament of Monsters', its 'anarchy and din Barbarian and informal' (*The Prelude*, Book VII). Lord Byron had a love–hate relationship with the city of his birth, enjoying living in high society there until domestic scandal forced him to flee abroad. From exile he denounced the city as a 'mighty Babylon'; in Canto X of his *Don Juan* (1823), Don Juan looks down from Shooter's Hill and sees

> A mighty mass of brick, and smoke, and shipping,
> Dirty and dusky, but as wide as eye
> Could reach, with here and there a sail just skipping
> In sight, then lost amidst the forestry
> Of masts: a wilderness of steeples peeping
> On tiptoe through their sea-coal canopy;
> A huge dun cupola, like a foolscap crown
> On a fool's head – and there is London Town.

City of Dreadful Night

The title of the Scottish poet James Thomson's 1874 poem 'City of Dreadful Night' is far better known than the poem itself, a long and leaden vision of urban dystopia. When Thomson was eight, his father's death and his mother's descent into melancholia led to his being placed in London's Royal Caledonian Asylum, where he came under the influence of millennial preachers. Educated at the Royal Military Academy, he became an army schoolmaster in Ireland before returning to London as a clerk and becoming a frequent visitor to the British Museum's reading room. Insomnia, alcoholism and chronic depression drove his pen in the writing of 'City of Dreadful Night', which drew its imagery from the New Testament books of Revelations and Corinthians, Dante's *Inferno* and Gustave Doré's stark illustrations for *London, A Pilgrimage* (a social commentary on the poor written by Blanchard Jerrold, and published in 1872). The poem is unmitigated gloom. London's inhabitants are 'the saddest and weariest men on earth' in a vortex where time is interminable and sleep unattainable. Faith, hope and charity are all dead; a River of Suicides runs through the city. 'There is no light behind the curtain ... all is vanity and nothingness.'

140

> Spectral night wanderers haunt the streets,
> Each adding poison to the poisoned air;
> Infections of unutterable sadness,
> Infections of incalculable madness,
> Infections of incurable despair.

A century and a half before Thomson, Daniel Defoe (c.1659–1731), a native Londoner, complained of the degeneracy of the city. In *Augusta Triumphans or, The Way to make London the Most Flourishing City in the Universe* (1728), he calls for the streets to be cleared of 'impudent strumpets'; for gaming tables and Sunday debauches to end; for the prevention of the 'immoderate use of Geneva [gin]'; and for the suppression of 'pretended Madhouses, where many of the Fair Sex are unjustly confined, while their Husbands keep Mistresses, etc, and many Widows are locked up for the sake of their jointure.'

Bedlam, London's ancient madhouse, appears in Tobias Smollett's *Humphrey Clinker* (1771) as a symbol of the city itself. To the Welsh squire Matthew Bramble the pleasure seekers in Vauxhall Gardens seem to be 'possessed by a spirit more absurd and pernicious than anything we meet in the precincts of Bedlam'. For Smollett the 'misshapen and monstrous capital' is 'without head or tail, members or proportion';

London

I wander thro' each dirty street
Near where the dirty Thames does flow
And ~~see~~ mark in every face I meet
Marks of weakness marks of woe

In every cry of every man
In every ~~infants cry of fear~~
~~In every voice of every child~~
In every voice in every ban
The ~~german~~ mind forg'd ~~links I hear~~ manacles I hear

~~How~~ the chimney sweepers cry
~~Blackens o'er the churches walls~~ Every blackning church appalls
And the hapless soldiers sigh
Runs in blood down palace walls

~~I slept~~ in the dark
In the silent night
I murmured my fears
And I felt delight

In the morning I went
As rosy as morn
To seek for new joy

But most the midnight harlots curse
From every dismal street I hear
Weaves around the marriage hearse
And blasts the new born infants tear
But most ~~the country~~ ~~in every street~~ I hear
How the midnight harlots curse
Blasts the new born infants tear
And hangs with plagues the marriage hearse

But most the shrieks of youth

When
And why
The
My
Then
And
Your
And you

Are now
Than
And as
Asham
Let ag
The
But
Pluck

46

142

it is an 'immense wilderness in which there is neither watch, nor ward of any signification, nor any order of police'.

William Blake, who lived in Lambeth from 1793 to 1800, wrote illustrated diatribes against the city's false sophistication, spiritual blindness, gradgrind education and glorification of machinery. He frequently saw apparitions: the Devil came up the stairs of his house in Hercules Street, Lambeth, and he conversed with 'the spiritual son' on Primrose Hill.

> Jerusalem came down in a dire rain over all the Earth,
> She felt cold from Lambeth's Vale in groans and dewy death –
> The dew of anxious souls, the death sweat of the dying –
> In every pillar'd hall and arch roof of Albion's skies.

Blake saw England, which he preferred to call Albion, as the battlefield of the forces of good and evil, dark and light. He published his poem 'London' in 1792, the year in which the French Revolution broke out. When the Parisian mob invaded the Tuileries and suspended the monarchy, Blake donned a red cap and cheered them on.

> I wander thro' each charter'd street,
> Near where the charter'd Thames does flow
> And mark in very face I meet
> Marks of weakness, marks of woe.
>
> In every cry of every Man,
> In every Infant's cry of fear,
> In every voice, in every ban
> The mind-forg'd manacles I hear.
>
> How the Chimney-sweepers cry
> Every blackening Church appalls,
> And the hapless Soldier's sigh
> Runs in blood down Palace walls.
>
> But most, thro' midnight streets I hear
> How the youthful Harlot's curse
> Blasts the new born Infant's tear,
> And blights with plagues the Marriage hearse.

143

OPPOSITE
'I wander thro' each charter'd street':
William Blake's 'London' as it appeared in his fantastically decorated *Songs of Experience*, 1794.

For vitriolic economy this poem takes some beating. The repetition of 'charter'd' in the first stanza emphasises the evil of private ownership – echoing the sentiments of

RIGHT
'Fire at Albion Mill', aquatint for Ackermann's *Microcosm of London*, 1808–10, from an original by Thomas Rowlandson. The much-hated mill, close to William Blake's Lambeth home, may have influenced his poem *Milton* which refers to 'dark satanic mills' and calls Satan the 'Miller of Eternity'.

Thomas Paine's *Rights of Man* (1791) which proclaims 'It is a perversion of terms to say that a charter gives rights. It operates by a contrary effect, that of taking rights away.' In the poem chimney-sweepers, soldiers and prostitutes are seen as exploited figures who represent threats to the established order. The last two lines of the third stanza refer to the revolutionary slogan 'No King' which had been daubed that year in red on the walls of the Privy Garden at Hampton Court, while the 'youthful harlot's curse' refers to the transmission of fatal venereal diseases to philandering husbands and through them to their wives and children.

The preface to Blake's *Milton* (1810) contains the poem 'Jerusalem', now a famous hymn, which celebrates a vision of Christ appearing in England and the freeing of humanity from the chains of commerce and war. It has been plausibly argued that its famous image of 'Dark Satanic Mills' was inspired by the much-hated steam-powered Albion Flour Mills, near Blackfriars Bridge. Later in *Milton*, Blake, who was living in nearby Lambeth, calls Satan 'the Miller of Eternity'. A spectacular fire, thought to have been caused by Luddite arson, destroyed the Albion Mills in 1791. 'The mob, who on all such occasions bestir themselves to extinguish a fire with that ready and disinterested activity which characterizes the English, stood by now as willing spectators of the conflagration,' reported the poet Robert Southey. The owners of wind and watermills waved placards which read 'Success to the Mills of ALBION but no Albion Mills'. The blackened shell of Albion Mills stood until 1809, when it was pulled down.

As the appalling state of the deprived districts of London was revealed by both government commissions and investigative journalists, more and more writers made the split nature of the city their concern. Foremost in popularity was Charles Dickens (1812–70). He experienced the streets of London intimately at an early age, walking from the family home in Camden Town to the Thameside blacking factory where he was sent to work as a boy, and he never lost his sympathy for the poor. Novels such as *Oliver Twist*, *Dombey and Son*, *Little Dorrit* and above all *Bleak House* painted London as a city that was morally and literally filthy and degenerate:

> Implacable November weather ... Smoke lowering down from chimney pots, making a soft black drizzle, with flakes of soot in it as big as full-grown snowflakes – gone into mourning, one might imagine, for the death of the sun ... Fog everywhere. Fog up the river, where it flows among green meadows; fog down the river, where it rolls defiled among the tiers of shipping and the waterside pollutions of a great (and dirty) city.

In 'Gin Shops', one of the series of articles depicting London scenes that were collected together in 1836 as *Sketches by 'Boz'*, Dickens described the 'filth, misery and squalor' of the slums close to Drury Lane, Holborn and Covent Garden, then contrasted them with the splendour of the gin-shops. 'What a change! All is light and brilliancy. The hum of many voices issues from that ... gay building with the fantastically ornamented parapet, the illuminated clock, the plate-glass windows surrounded by stucco rosettes and its profusion of gas-lights in richly-gilt burners, is perfectly dazzling'. An elegantly carved bar of French mahogany extends the width of the room, and two side aisles hold 'great casks, painted green and gold'. The clientele is mixed: two old washerwomen humbly sip 'half-quarters of gin and peppermint'; a young man about town flirts with the barmaid; 'a female in faded feathers' explains that 'this gentleman pays', and 'calls for a glass of port wine and a bit of sugar'. Two old men make themselves 'crying drunk' and a fat comfortable elderly woman stands a round of rum-scrub, 'saying "as good people's wery [sic] scarce, what I says is, make the most on [sic] 'em"'. Towards the end of the evening a band of Irish labourers begin a fight; the police are called in and the evening dissolves into chaos.

George Gissing (1857–1903) gave to the bleakest of his London slum novels the title *The Nether World* (1889) – a phrase taken from Henry Cary's 1805 translation of Dante. It starts and ends in graveyards.

ABOVE
A quarrel breaks out between two drunken street women under the glittering façade of a gin-shop in Seven Dials. George Cruikshank's illustration for Charles Dickens' first book, *Sketches by 'Boz' Illustrative of Everyday Life and Everyday People* (1836).

Here on the waste limits of the dread east, to wander among tombs is to go hand in hand with the stark and eyeless emblems of mortality; the spirit fails beneath the cold burden of ignoble destiny.

There is a gruesome description of a daemonic stone effigy set in the arch of the Middlesex House of Detention (Gissing himself served a prison sentence for theft early in his life), while the descriptions of the 'squalid and toil-infested' slums are peppered with real names. When planning the book, Gissing wandered the streets of Clerkenwell over several weeks. 'I have something in hand which I hope to turn to some vigorous purpose,' he wrote to Thomas Hardy, 'a story that has grown up in recent ramblings about Clerkenwell – dark, but with evening sunlight at the close.' Dark it certainly was, much influenced by the sordid death of Gissing's wife, a former prostitute whom he had moved heaven and earth to save, but failed to prevent dying from a combination of drink and syphilis.

The illustrated and still rousingly readable weekly pamphlets known as 'penny-dreadfuls' or 'penny-bloods' were as influential as anything by Dickens or Gissing in trumpeting London horrors. George Reynolds (1814–79), who excelled at these fast-moving fictions, also edited *Reynolds' Miscellany of Romance, General Literature, Science, and Art*, a periodical dedicated to improving the popular mind. Reynolds was a Chartist, and the lurid stories in his *Mysteries of London* series (1844–7) emphasised upper-class debauchery and lower-class miseries. The first tale opens on 'a dark and stormy night' and tells the story of a wealthy young man who misses his way and finds himself lost in Smithfield, 'like a flower on a foetid manure-heap'. In its preface, Reynolds declares that in London

> The most unbounded wealth is the neighbour of the most hideous poverty ... the crumbs which fall from the tables of the rich would appear delicious viands to starving millions, and yet these millions obtain them not! In that city there are in all five prominent buildings: the church, in which the pious pray; the gin-palace, to which the wretched poor resort to drown their sorrows; the pawn-broker's, where miserable creatures pledge their raiment, and their children's raiment, even unto the last rag, to obtain the means of purchasing food, and – alas! too often – intoxicating drink; the prison, where the victims of a vitiated condition of society expiate the crimes to which they have been driven by starvation and despair; and the workhouse, to which the destitute, the aged, and the friendless hasten to lay down their aching heads – and die!

Two notorious murderers haunt the minds of London's more ghoulish writers, one fictional, one real. Sweeney Todd, the murdering robber-barber of Fleet Street, was invented by James Rymer and Thomas Peckett. The two authors wrote alternate instalments, each more shocking than the last, of an 18-part penny-dreadful series called *The String of Pearls: A Romance* (1846–7). The sheer horror of the plot, and the ingenuity of the revolving trapdoor under the barber's chair, which despatched its doomed occupants to dismemberment and baking in Mrs Levett's nearby pie shop, seized artistic imaginations. Among the spin-offs have been numerous plays and songs, a ballet scored by Matthew Arnold, a musical by Stephen Sondheim, films by John Schlesinger and Tim Burton and an unfinished graphic comic by Neil Gaiman.

Jack the Ripper was the name given to a serial killer of East End prostitutes in the late 1880s. Never identified, he specialised in mutilating their abdominal organs. The obsession with the eleven cases grouped together as 'the Whitechapel Murders' amounted to a media feeding frenzy. 'Ripperology' still fascinates: books galore have been, and continue to be, written, as do poems, plays, operas, television dramas and films. Alan Moore's comic book series *From Hell* (1991) took its title from the heading of a particularly dark letter, purporting to be from the killer himself, and enclosing a kidney supposedly obtained from one of the victims. Stewart Home's *Down and Out in Shoreditch and Hoxton* (2004), a slice-and-dice novel reflecting the influence of William Burroughs, features a remarkably learned whore called Eve who debates the nature of prostitution and fingers authors galore as possible murderers. Weighing up the likelihood of Henry James or George Gissing being Jack the Ripper, the book concludes that he was in fact Bruce Chatwin. Home wrote with the Twitter-like limitation that every paragraph should be exactly 100 words long.

The enduring speculation that Jack the Ripper was an upper- or middle-class gentleman who went slumming for his murderous kicks may have had its roots in the appearance of Robert Louis Stevenson's *Strange Case of Dr Jekyll and Mr Hyde* in 1886. Stevenson was fascinated by the idea of the *doppelganger*, using it in his tale as a symbolic representation of what Henry James, who admired the book, called 'the

RIGHT
Sweeney Todd, the murderous villain of James Rymer and Thomas Peckett's gory penny-dreadful serial *The String of Pearls* (1846–7) seized the popular imagination, and the story was retold countless times. Title page of George Dibdin Pitt's play 'Sweeney Todd: the Barber of Fleet Street', 1883.

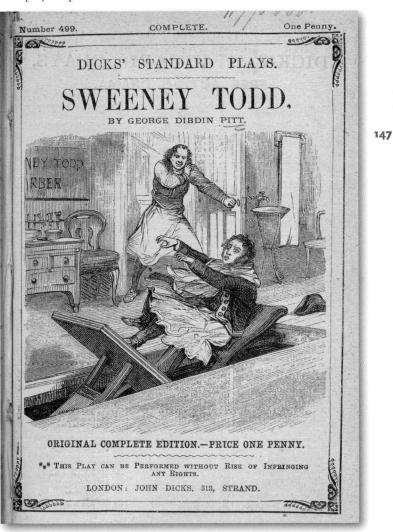

Number 499.   COMPLETE.   One Penny.

DICKS' STANDARD PLAYS.

SWEENEY TODD.

BY GEORGE DIBDIN PITT.

ORIGINAL COMPLETE EDITION.—PRICE ONE PENNY.

** THIS PLAY CAN BE PERFORMED WITHOUT RISK OF INFRINGING ANY RIGHTS.

LONDON: JOHN DICKS, 313, STRAND.

BELOW
Robert Louis
Stevenson portrayed
London as 'a city in a
nightmare', as divided
as the title characters
in *The Strange Case of
Dr Jekyll and Mr Hyde*.
S. G. Hulme Beaman
drew this illustration
of Mr Hyde murdering
Sir Danvers Carew for
an edition of 1930.

perpetual moral question ... the difficulty of being good and the brutishness of being bad'. Stevenson created an equally divided London backdrop, well-lit and prosperous in scenes with Dr Jekyll, menacing and fog-filled when Jekyll's puzzled lawyer Utterson searches for the 'troglodytic and wicked-looking' Hyde, little suspecting that he is the alter ego of his patrician client.

A great chocolate-coloured pall lowered over heaven, but the wind was continually charging and routing these embattled vapours ... The dismal quarter of Soho seen under these changing glimpses, with its muddy ways, and slatternly passengers, and its lamps ... kindled afresh to combat this mournful reinvasion of darkness, seemed in the lawyer's eyes, like a district of some city in a nightmare.

The Welsh writer and mystic Arthur Machen (1863–1947) went much further than Stevenson in his notorious – and instantly condemned – novella *The Great God Pan* (1894). It relates the story of how Helen Vaughan, a monstrous but apparently beautiful

offspring of an innocent Welsh girl and Pan himself (here made unutterably terrible, in no way resembling Kenneth Grahame's protective spirit of nature), comes to London, settles in Soho and ruins the young men who fall in love with her. 'London has been called the city of encounters; it is more than that, it is the city of Resurrections,' muses the book's hero Villiers, just before he meets the wreck of Herbert, an old friend who is one of Helen's many victims. 'You may think you know life, and London, and what goes on day and night in this dreadful city ... but I tell you you can have no conception of what I know, not in your most fantastic, hideous dreams.'

Popular dread of anarchist outrages in 1890s London lay behind Joseph Conrad's *The Secret Agent* (1907), but the book also emphasises the existence of a dark underworld, in this case a revolutionary one. Verloc, a slothful and domesticated Soho shopkeeper, is secretly taking payments from the Russian embassy to encourage outrages by communist activists in London. Dissatisfied with his inertia, the embassy requires him to prove his loyalty by bombing Greenwich Observatory, a plot inspired by an attempt to do just that by a suicide bomber in 1894. Conrad's descriptions of London's streets are pregnant with doom, above all in the scene when Mrs Verloc, devastated by the death of her brother ('blown to fragments in a state of innocence'), stabs her supine husband and heads for the oblivion of the Thames:

It was not actually raining, but each gas lamp had a rusty little halo of mist. The van and horses were gone, and in the black street the curtained window of the carters' eating-house made a square patch of soiled blood-red light glowing faintly very near the level of the pavement ... She was alone in London: and the whole town of marvels and mud, with its maze of streets and its mass of lights, was sunk in a hopeless night, rested at the bottom of a black abyss from which no unaided woman could hope to scramble out.

Street Haunting

When writers walked London's streets, they excavated its past in their imaginations and presented their own versions of its present. Daniel Defoe, William Blake, Charles Dickens and George Gissing all gathered material for their criticisms of the London of their day by exploring its underside on foot. The Elizabethan John Stow (c.1525–1603) was by contrast an urban archaeologist, methodically cataloguing highways and byways, mansions, churches and bridges out of national pride, giving lengthy pedigrees of occupants ancient and modern. His *Survey of London* (1598) is now seen as a seminal text by 'psychogeographers', modern city-dwellers who enjoy roaming at random around the urban environment and developing new ways of experiencing it in words and images.

Thomas de Quincey (1785–1859) loved London, which he first saw when he was only 15. When he described his 'peregrinations' around London as a vulnerable teenager in *Confessions of an English Opium-Eater* (1821), he emphasises the kindness of strangers: a shady lawyer, a 15-year-old prostitute, a fellow-traveller on a coach and his aristocratic young friend, Lord Altamont. He was desperately poor while living in London, sheltering in an all but empty Oxford Street house with only a 10-year-old servant girl for companionship; in a digression which jumps the reader into his more prosperous (but still peregrinating) present, he describes walking past the same house 18 years later: 'It is now occupied by a respectable family, and, by the lights of the front drawing-room, I observed a domestic party, assembled perhaps at tea, and apparently cheerful and gay.'

De Quincey only feels alienated from the bustling humanity of the city when he starts to take opium to heighten his experiences of city markets and the

149

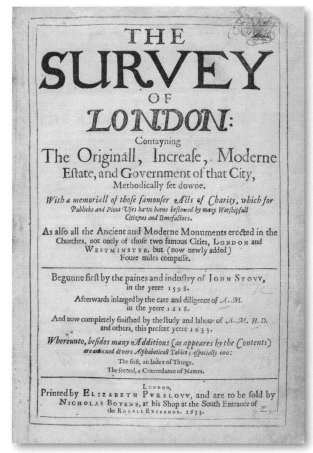

THE
SURVEY
OF
LONDON:
Contayning
The Originall, Increase, Moderne
Estate, and Government of that City,
Methodically set downe.

With a memoriall of those famouse Acts of Charity, which for Publicke and Pious Uses have beene bestowed by many Worshipfull Citizens and Benefactors.

As also all the Ancient and Moderne Monuments erected in the Churches, not onely of those two famous Cities, LONDON and WESTMINSTER, but (now newly added) Foure miles compasse.

Begunne first by the paines and industry of IOHN STOVV, in the yeere 1598.
Afterwards inlarged by the care and diligence of A. M. in the yeere 1618.
And now completely finished by the study and labour of A. M. H. D. and others, this present yeere 1633.

Whereunto, besides many Additions (as appeares by the Contents) are annexed divers Alphabeticall Tables; especially two:
The first, an Index of Things.
The second, a Concordance of Names.

LONDON,
Printed by ELIZABETH PVRSLOVV, and are to be sold by
NICHOLAS BOVRNE, at his Shop at the South Entrance of
the ROYALL EXCHANGE. 1633.

opera. Then dreams and visions mingle with reality, and London's labyrinthine nature becomes a recurring theme. Trying to find his way home after an opium-tinged Saturday night outing, he tries to steer 'upon nautical principles, by fixing my eye on the pole-star ... I came suddenly upon such knotty problems as alleys, such enigmatical entries, and such sphinx's riddles of streets without thoroughfares ... I could almost have believed, at times, that I was the first discoverer of some of these *terrae incognitae*, and doubted whether they had yet been laid down in the modern charts of London ... The perplexities of my steps came back and haunted my sleep.'

He was frank and unashamed that his closest companion was a young prostitute called Ann.

> Being at that time of necessity a peripatetic, or a walker of the streets, I naturally fell in more frequently with those female peripatetics who are technically called Street-walkers ... It may well be supposed that in the existing state of my purse, my connexion with such women could not have been an impure one. But the truth is that at no time in my life have I been a person to hold myself polluted by the touch or approach of any creature that wore a human shape.

Their friendship came to an end when de Quincey left London, and he never found her again, often as he haunted their customary meeting place in Great Titchfield Street. He imagines Ann also searching for him 'in the mighty labyrinths of London', where 'even a street's width amounted to a separation for eternity'.

Charles Dickens devoted an essay to midnight prowls. In *Night Walks* (1869), he conjures up a city made unfamiliar and menacing by its dark emptiness. Making his way into a deserted theatre, 'the rows of faces faded out, the lights extinguished, and the seats all empty', he looked into the orchestra pit which appeared 'like a great grave dug for a time of pestilence'. He then went on to Newgate, lingering by 'that wicked little Debtors' Door ... which has been Death's Door to so many'. Later he passed by Bethlehem Hospital (the notorious Bedlam),

> because I had a night fancy in my head that could be best pursued within sight of its walls and dome. And the fancy was this: Are not the sane and the insane equal at night as the sane lie dreaming? Are not all of us outside this hospital who dream, more or less in the condition of those inside it, every night of our lives?

Crossing over graveyards he thought of the 'enormous hosts of the dead', and how, if they were raised while the living slept, 'there would not be the space of a pin's point in all the streets and ways for the living to come out into'.

Although London was portrayed as a quagmire of iniquity and menace by some

OPPOSITE
Street-haunting
Londoners like Thomas
de Quincey, Charles
Dickens and Henry
James found the nether
regions of the city
labyrinthine and
fascinating, but also
melancholy and
menacing. St Mary
Overy's Dock, *c*.1881.
Photographed by
Henry Dixon for
the Society of
Photographing Relics
of Old London.

151

BELOW
In his late teens and early twenties, Arthur Ransome struggled to make a living as a writer in pre-First World War London. This illustration by Fred Taylor for Ransome's autobiographical *Bohemia in London* (1907) shows the bookshops in the Charing Cross Road from which he built up a library.

authors, to others its streets offered a richly rewarding cornucopia of culture and entertainment. Henry James (1843–1916) brilliantly pinpointed the contradictions of 'the murky, modern Babylon' in his 1905 essay, 'London'. Approaching by train from Liverpool, he admired its immensity, 'the miles of housetops and viaducts, the complications of junctions and signals'. A subsequent walk along the Strand 'was the commencement of my passion ... It struck me as desirable, even indispensable, that I should purchase most of the articles in most of the shops.' But a few days later, alone in inhospitable lodgings, 'an impersonal black hole in the huge general blackness',

> a sudden horror of the whole place came over me, like a tiger-pounce of homesickness which had been watching its moment. London was hideous, vicious, cruel, and above all, overwhelming ... It appeared to me that I would rather remain dinnerless, would rather even starve, than sally forth into that infernal town, where the natural fate of an obscure stranger would be to be trampled to death in Piccadilly and his carcass thrown in the Thames. I did not starve, however, and I eventually attached myself by a hundred human links to the dreadful, delightful city.

In the 1900s Arthur Ransome (1884–1967) was a well-established London reviewer and essayist. The writer of critical studies of both Robert Louis Stevenson and Oscar Wilde, he also loved walking the city streets, becoming one of the first writers to map London by its authors, artists and poets. His *Bohemia in London* (1907) is spun as fictional, but the places are real, and the characters he visits are in the main easily identifiable – the sculptor Jacob Epstein, the novelist M.P. Shiel, the poet Edward

THE BOOKSTALLS OF THE CHARING CROSS ROAD

Thomas. Nothing is more vivid than his chapter on the 'Bookshops of Bohemia'. He imagines a host of earlier 'street readers': John Gay 'walking "with sweet content on foot, wrapped in his virtue and a good surtout"' to browse the books on the Charing Cross bookstalls, and Charles Lamb doing the same, 'filching a little learning' with 'fearful joy'. The book is almost uncannily lacking in any consciousness of the deprivation of the masses beyond the charmed upper echelons; poverty for Ransome is going short of food in order to buy more books. He was much influenced by such cheerful and generally optimistic London-based essayists as William Hazlitt and Thomas Hood.

Virginia Woolf (1882–1941) combined Ransome's cheerfulness with an acknowledgement of the city's darker side in her 1930 essay 'Street Haunting', a subtly constructed 'London Adventure'. It begins with a playful urge to be on the move, indulging 'in the greatest pleasure of town life ... rambling the streets of London.'

> The hour should be the evening and the season winter, for in winter the champagne brightness of the air and the sociability of the streets are grateful ... The evening hour, too, gives us the responsibility which darkness and lamplight bestow. We are no longer quite ourselves. As we step out of the house on a fine evening between four and six, we shed the self our friends know us by and become part of that vast republican army of anonymous trampers.

After praising the beauty of lamplit squares and the 'glossy brilliance of motor-omnibuses' as she strolls towards the Strand on the spurious errand of buying a pencil, Woolf begins to introduce a different perspective – people who are 'humped, twisted, deformed', 'an old woman flung abandoned on the step of a public building with a cloak over her like the hasty covering thrown over a dead horse or donkey'. She deliberately flips from light to shadow and back again, skimming over surface appearances then delving into the emotions behind the human shells of those she encounters. The essay reveals the workings of a great novelist's mind: 'Into each of these lives one could penetrate a little way ... And what greater delight and wonder can there be than to leave the straight lines of personality and deviate into those footpaths that lead beneath brambles and thick tree-trunks into the heart of the forest where live those wild beasts, our fellow men?'

Woolf confronts London's literary past as well as its everyday present. She is reminded of Defoe when she looks out over the Thames: 'The view of London from Hungerford Bridge, grey, serious, massive, and full of the subdued stir of traffic and business, prosaic if it were not for the masts of the ships and the towers and domes of the city, brings him to mind. The tattered girls with violets in their hands at the street corners, and the old weather-beaten women patiently displaying their matches and bootlaces beneath the shelter of the arches, seem like characters from his books' (*The Common Reader*, 1925).

The main characters in Woolf's *Mrs Dalloway*, also published in 1925, wander the streets and parks of London to the regular striking of clocks. Clarissa Dalloway herself is a street saunterer, rather than a haunter; she walks the city with a Joycean combination of outward observation and internal musing. 'What a lark! What a plunge!' she exclaims to herself as she waits at the kerb on her way to Bond Street to buy flowers for her evening party. The tragic Septimus, by contrast, is tormented by suicidal thoughts as his desperate wife leads him into Regent's Park. Originally to be called *The Hours*, the novel adopts the stream of consciousness approach. Its characters cross the same spaces but at different times, and all are deep in memories of the past.

In her last book Angela Carter (1940–92) showed her deep love of London in *Wise Children* (1991) – a carnivalesque story of twin theatrical burlesque artists Dora and Nora Chance. Illegitimate children of the larger-than-life Shakespearean actor Melchior Hazard, the Chance twins live in a rambling house in Brixton, described by Dora as 'the bastard side of Old Father Thames' – as much on the 'wrong side' of the river as they are on the 'wrong side of the blanket'. But the twins are unashamed, rejoicing in living in the city's hybrid and vibrant underside, and enjoying crossing the river to visit their father's West End mansion. Dora, the book's narrator, is fascinated by the sense of things changed, and things still changing. She looks out of her window and tells us that

> You can see for miles, out of this window. You can see straight across the river. There's Westminster Abbey, see? Flying the St. George's cross, today. St. Paul's, the single breast. Big Ben, winking its golden eye. Not much else familiar, these days. This is about the time that comes in every century when they reach out for all that they can grab of dear old London, and pull it down. Then they build it up again, like London Bridge in the nursery rhyme, goodbye, hello, but it's never the same. Even the railway stations, changed out of recognition, turned into souks. Waterloo, Victoria. Nowhere you can get a decent cup of tea, all they give you is Harvey Wallbangers, filthy cappuccino. Stocking shops and knicker outlets everywhere you look. I said to Nora: 'Remember *Brief Encounter*, how I cried buckets? Nowhere for them to meet on a station, nowadays, except in a bloody knicker shop. Their hands would have to shyly touch under cover of a pair of Union Jack boxer shorts.'

Neil Gaiman's *Neverwhere* (1996) is a tongue-in-cheek modern fantasy that harks back to Victorian gothic and the theme of London's divided nature. He spins a mythic story around London Above and London Below, with Underground stations personified as rulers of the fiefs of a complexly imagined parallel underworld. An awesome Angel

OPPOSITE
Tower bells sounding the hours and the half-hours punctuate the London roamings of the characters in Virginia Woolf's *Mrs Dalloway*, and she originally called the novel *The Hours*. Mrs Dalloway is the epitome of the urban walker, who creates the city as she walks it: 'making it up, building it round one, tumbling it, creating it every moment afresh'. Shown here is page 5 from Woolf's original manuscript (1923–25).

5

June 29th 1923.

The Hours.

In Westminster, where temples, meeting houses, conventicles, & steeples of all kinds are congregated together, there is, at all hours & half hours, a round of bells, connecting correcting each other, asseverating that time has come a little earlier, or stayed a little later, here or here. Thus when Mr. Walsh walking with his head a little down, & his coat flying loose came out by the Abbey the clock of St Margarets was saying two minutes later than Big Ben that it was half past eleven. But her voice was a womans voice, since its impossible to have anything to do with inanimate objects without giving them sex; & the very stair rods have character, & their fate send them to the old furniture shops — their owners spun by their voices would be heard in their own accents bringing back countless passages up & down stairs, moments too of happiness, or despair, moments not otherwise communicable, for there has attached itself even to the stair rod, something that lies below words.

St Margarets spoke as a woman speaks, their way with a vibration in the core of the round so that with some that each word, or note, comes fluttering, alive, yet with some reluctance to inflict its vitality, some grief for the past which holds it back, some impulse nevertheless to glide into the waves of the heart & there bury itself in ring after ring of sound, so that Mr. Walsh, as he walked past St Margarets, & heard the bells toll the half hour felt ....

of all that surrounded it, of its futility. For he had never married her.   He had failed.   But he now loved more passionately than then. His first in India ..... He had been sent down from Oxford. He had drunk two ... he had been a socialist. But the future of the

One.   *The proletariat.*

not that it's done any good to the buses, has it, they've all got they sweep past the rain-drenched queues in their fucking Porsches mocking don't they.

Q.   Why is London like Budapest?

A.   Because it is two cities divided by a river.

Once upon a time, you could

You ~~used to be able to~~ make a crude distinction, thus: the rich lived
on the North bank, amongst pleasant verdure ~~and exclusive shopping to~~ α
~~which they were~~ whisked *to exclusive shopping* by abundant public transport, while the poor
eked out miserable existences on the South bank in circumstances of arid
deprivation, condemned, if they wanted some release from their transpontine
limbo, to wait for hours at wind-swept bus stops whilst ~~partially feral cats~~
~~noisily marauded dustinbs~~ filled with cans already scraped bare, ~~and~~ the
sounds of marital violence offended ~~the~~ cold, dark air ~~where~~ *whereon there* hung the greasy
ghosts of ~~yesterday's~~ *yestreen's* fish and chips. *(Note that beat; that's an iambic pentameter - see? Sound* p.t.o.

diesel Saatoa Porsches, & the devil take the rest.

& α creaking glass

& now no buses anywhere They ... by ... speed by in their Volvo estates

But you ~~cant~~ can't trust anything, these days; you ~~can't trust the~~
~~rich to stay~~ ~~xgax~~ ~~where it's good for them~~ *in their place but* , ~~not x since they treated~~
~~themselves to Porchses.~~ There's ~~bn~~ been a gigantic diaspora of the
affluent. ~~The rich have been~~ *They* scattered all over the city; that's what
happens when property values go through the roof.

And what does the robin do then, poor thing.

Had the sense to invest in a ... of brick & mortar, &, most of all, freehold,

Bugger the robin. What would have become of us? If ~~our mum~~ *our gran* hadn't ~~had the~~
~~had the snese to buy this house,~~ ~~knock down~~ price on account of the
~~blitz,~~ we'd be out on the streets, now, Nora and me, pushing our worldlies
up and down on supermarket trollies, reduced to sucking on the bottle
for comfort like babes unweaned the day our giros came in ~~and x~~ whilst
intermittently bursting into song to relieve x our anguish, *to* embarking
upon ecstatic arias out of pure joy and relief when finally we gained
entrance to the blessed night shelter and therefore chucked out for
disturbing the peace to gasp and wheeze and freeze on the midnight
street.

Bless this house

& snuff out ... it penny candle ... the end.

presides at Islington, a bucolic Earl holds medieval Court, and Night's Bridge has no smart shops at all, just a murderous darkness. When Richard Mayhew (a resonant amalgamation of Dick Whittington and Henry Mayhew, chronicler of the capital's Victorian slums) goes to the Downside, the smoke-filled hall he discovers, full of shadowy people in fur-trimmed rags 'roasting small animals on spits', is straight from the engravings of Cruikshank and Doré.

Neverwhere began as a BBC television series, but the later novel gave more scope to tell the story as Gaiman had originally envisaged it. For all its dark moments, we never doubt that its heroes Richard and Door, child of good magic, will prevail; the same is true of Gaiman's audacious fantasy for children *The Graveyard Book* (2008), the story of a toddler symbolically called Nobody Owens who survives the murderous onslaught of a killer called Jack Frost on his family by wandering into a graveyard. The tale is a black but wise and ultimately benign take on Rudyard Kipling's allegory of growing up, *The Jungle Book*. The hilltop cemetery with its spiked iron railings, stone angels, tombs and an obelisk to an eminent brewer is recognisably one of London's solemn, high Victorian resting places for the dead, and in this case undead. Jack proves to be 'a beast of prey', both an evocation of the Ripper and a member of the threatening gangs that rule London's underworld; tendrils of fog straight from a Sherlock Holmes story by Conan Doyle thread their way through the tale.

Today London is a territory exhaustively tramped by 'psychogeographers' seeking to knit its past with its future, its ancient myths and its sordid modern realities. These latter-day Resurrection men find stimulus in the enduring nature of its names – villages enveloped by its sprawling suburbs, churches celebrating forgotten saints and pubs: the Brazen Head, the Green Man, The Sun in Splendour, the Bear and Ragged Staff. Their approach was anticipated by B.S. Johnson (1933–73). In *Albert Angelo* (1964), Albert, an architect manqué condemned to work as a supply teacher in turbulent classrooms, experiences the pretentious portico of his parents' Victorian terrace house as the opening scene of a film. Johnson's description of Albert's wanderings through London, studying faces and architectural details with a critical gaze, is like a succession of photographs.

> I wonder, shall I come to accept St Pancras station, living so near? Or even to like it? Perhaps it is fatal to live so near St Pancras station for an architect. Certainly it would be to bring up children here: their aesthetic would be blighted.

Johnson employs metaphors from architecture to describe the people Albert sees, which gives a coolness and distance to his reflections. Sex is important in the novel, but it is itemised in forensic, deliberately unarousing detail. Johnson's style switches abruptly: play dialogue, first person narrative, second person narrative, nostalgic reflections on a lost girlfriend (punningly named Jenny Taylor) and, famously, a

OPPOSITE
'Q. Why is London like Budapest? A. Because it is two cities divided by a river.' Angela Carter's typescript of the opening page of her ebullient tale of twin vaudeville artists, *Wise Children* (1991) showing her revisions.

slot cut out of page 147 to provide a glimpse of words that apparently forewarn of violence ahead, which we assume will involve one of Albert's pupils:

struggled to take back his knife, and inflicted on him a mortal wound above his right eye (the blade penetrating to a depth of two inches) from which he died instantly

The lines are in fact from a report on the death in a London tavern of the Elizabethan playwright Christopher Marlowe. Past is brought into present. Albert's final truth is 'sitting here writing looking out across Claremont Square trying to say something about the writing and nothing being an answer to the loneliness to the lack of loving'. In the end, he rejects his own 'pretty parallels' between the 'built-on-the-skew, tatty, half-complete, comically-called Percy Circus, and Albert, and London, and England, and the human condition'.

London itself, as well as the Thames, is the chosen territory of the Hackney-based writer Iain Sinclair (b.1943); attacking its exploiters and exploring its myths is his obsession. In the 1970s Sinclair, an admirer not only of Allen Ginsberg and Jack Kerouac but also of William Blake, immersed himself in punk hippiedom, drugs, ley lines and black magic before writing his *Lud Heat* (1975), in which London's old buildings and churches reveal their history in hallucinogenic flashes. The time-travelling hero of *Slow Chocolate Autopsy* (1998) witnesses murders from Marlowe to McVitie; *Lights Out for the Territory: 9 Excursions in the Secret History of London* fantasises about encounters with Dalston hoods, feral dogs, the Kray brothers and Lord Archer; the American critic Melissa Rossi described it as 'like a high-speed ride in a stolen car – images recklessly thrown before you, then knocked over by sheer velocity as you pass'.

In recent years Sinclair has abandoned the novel in favour of recording both on film and in words his meanderings, encounters and opinions. *London: City of Disappearances* (2006) is an amorphous anthology of reflections, stories, protests and memories by Sinclair's 'friends and friends of friends', who were given the brief to write about things that were or had already disappeared. They are credited after each

ABOVE
The tower blocks and rundown streets of Hackney and Dalston are the chosen territory of Iain Sinclair's psychogeographic literary experiments. Photograph taken from a canal bridge on the New North Road looking East.

OPPOSITE
Page 147 of
B.S. Johnson's
experimental novel
Albert Angelo (1964)
has a slot cut through
several pages of text in
order to give the reader
a misleading glimpse
of future events.

"Give with the reechy kisses, babe," said Albert.

"Kindly get stuffed," said the waitress.

"Only time I did touch them, hurt them," Albert resumed, "was today, for the first time. I was giving a bloody brilliant lesson on architecture—it was brilliant, too—and the bastards still weren't paying attention and still mucked about, and I lost my temper and said they were a lot of peasants. That they resented, being called peasants, that touched them, that hurt them. They copied chunks out of the Bible for the rest of the lesson, and I could feel the resentment in the room. It wasn't the copying out of the Bible, I'm sure, they probably hated that less than me rabbitting on about architecture, but being called peasants. Perhaps it has country bumpkin associations for London kids? Strange that it should be the only thing to touch them. But you know what I've decided to do in the last few days of term? I'm going to give them time and paper to write down exactly what they feel about me, with a guarantee that there will be no complaints or recriminations from me, whatever they say. This I hope will work out their hatred of me without it actually needing to come to violence. How about that for an idea, then?"

* * * * *

struggled to take back his knife, and mortal wound above his right eye (the blade to a depth of two inches) from which he died passage and more fully identified at the end of the book. Marina Warner explores pubs called after legendary hags; Paul Buck haunts the Charing Cross bookshops and Will Self offers a deliberately chilling but also luminously evocative description of the 'Brutalist aspiration' of the Nine Elms Cold Store. For good measure Thomas de Quincey, a favourite of Sinclair's, gets a look in with his fruitless quest for his friend Ann of Oxford Street. Sinclair describes the books as a 'deflected autobiography, scripted by an automatic pen in an end-of-the-pier booth in an out-of-season resort'; the passages are 'the missing chapters of a book I was incapable of writing'.

'He Do the Police in Different Voices'

T. S. Eliot's *The Waste Land* (1922) was originally called 'He Do The Police in Different Voices' – a reference to Sloppy in Dickens's *Our Mutual Friend*, who reads out newspaper accounts of London crimes. The poem is itself an impressionistic portrait of the collective psyche after the First World War, and London voices weave through it, both those of casually glimpsed strangers and such long-dead authors as Spenser and Dickens, Chaucer and Conrad. Different voices are the soundtrack of modern London. The science fiction writer Michael Moorcock's *Mother London* (1988) tells the story of London from the Blitz to the 1980s through a chorus of contrasted voices from the past heard in the deluded minds of three outpatients from a mental hospital. Cockney, he announces at the end of the book, is the original language of the world. Will Self takes this fantasy further in *The Book of Dave* (2006), the story of a post-apocalyptic 'Nú Lundun' in which people speak either a demotic 'Mokni' or, for official duties, 'Arpee' [Received Pronunciation]. Taxi routes are the new liturgy: '4wd Kenzingtun Mal, rî Kenzungtun Chirch Stree, leff Nó-ing-ill, rí, rí Pemrij Röd'.

'The past is a country from which we have all emigrated, its loss is part of our common humanity,' says Salman Rushdie in *Imaginary Homelands* (1991). 'The writer who is out-of-country and even out-of-language may experience this loss in an intensified form.' A remarkable literature has been developed in the half-century since the arrival of the *Empress Windrush* from the West Indies. Since London became the home of these New Britons, its landscape and their experiences in it have naturally been a primary source of inspiration. Trinidad-born Sam Selvon (1923–94) set *The Lonely Londoners* (1956) in the Harrow Road and Bayswater. Made the more powerful by being told in creolised patois, it is a poignant account of the disappointment of the optimistic Caribbean immigrants. 'This city powerfully lovely when you on your own,' says its hero Moses Aloetta, but 'nobody does really accept you.' Aloetta makes it his business to haunt Waterloo station in order to help other immigrants, despite the overwhelming sensation of homesickness it gives him. 'For the old Waterloo station is a place of arrival and departure, is a place where you see people crying goodbye and kissing welcome, and he hardly have time to sit down on a bench before this feeling of nostalgia hit him and he was surprise'.

OPPOSITE
'Nobody does really accept you': The world of Sam Selvon's *Lonely Londoners* is evoked by Bert Hardy's 1949 photograph for a *Picture Post* article called 'Is there a British colour bar?'

160

Zadie Smith's *White Teeth* (2000) is a many-layered account of multi-cultural London and the trials and tribulations of mixed-race marriages. 'What is past is prologue' is its opening line, and it is written from multiple viewpoints and in varied voices. Among them are the middle-aged English Archie, who marries a Jamaican, his Bangladeshi wartime friend Samad, the Jewish Oxford geneticist Marcus Chalfen and Samad's Bangladesh-educated fundamentalist Muslim son Milat, a representative of the new 'Black British' generation. Teeth are its leitmotif, symbolising the unifying of the cultures through the integration of spoken language, the stabilising of hybrid senses of self, through language, words and action.

Gautam Malkani's novel *Londonstani* (2006) is about young South Asians who wander from stealing mobile phones into gangland crime; for good measure there is a Romeo and Juliet romance between a Hindu boy and a Muslim girl. It is written in an intriguing mixture of English, Punjabi, Urdu, obscenities, rap and textspeak. Flawed as a novel, it is nevertheless a clever and accurate mirror of the new Babel that is London today.

Chap 1   (1)

Asleep ~~Secure~~ Astley The suburbs dream of violence. ~~Asleep~~ ~~kindly~~ in their drowsy villas, ~~secure~~ sheltered by ~~benevolent/generous~~ their ~~grateful~~ shopping malls, they wait for the ~~(kindly)~~ nightmares that will wake them into a more ~~real~~ passionate world ~~moved at his him~~

(A) (B) (C) & As I ~~whenever I had~~ looked

~~[they had felt this for years]~~

down from the motorway at the airport ~~Heathrow~~

~~contented~~ Here we were ~~the contented~~ flatlands beyond ~~the Planetary rim, they look quite mystery~~ the [Suburban townns few people could give a name to, and which featured on noone's mental maps. No one ~~showed ever be this content.~~ by night

~~What could rouse them from their~~

~~concrete mattress and send them~~

~~the workers to their garden gates?~~

~~twitching foolish thoughts~~ I Told ~~Harris~~ Took

fantasies ~~amiable~~ (Stories) ~~thing~~ Londoner

BEYOND THE CITY

Urban Outskirts

Beyond the safety of the medieval city's walls were its 'outskirts', home of the poor and those of low repute who were not admitted to the privilege of citizenship. The district of Southwark, on the south side of the Thames, though not yet as sleazy as it would become, was notorious even in Chaucer's day for the prostitutes only allowed to ply their trade beyond the city's walls. In the 'Canon's Yeoman's Tale', Chaucer makes it clear that the Canon and his man, who chase after the pilgrims with a haste that suggests a flight, were staying close to the Tabard, the Southwark inn at which his Canterbury pilgrims gathered before their journey.

The sweating Canon wears a filthy, torn coat, and his garrulous yeoman reveals that he is an alchemist; the pair scrape a living by pretending to be able to double in quantity any gold they are given. When the Host asks where they live, the yeoman replies

> In the outskirts of a city ...
> In corners and blind alleyways we lurk
> Where all your thieves by nature do their work,
> Reside in secrecy and fear, from where
> They dare not show their faces.

By the 1600s, the lure of the city had enticed so many to its suburbs that James I complained that 'soon London will be all England'. 'How happy therefore were cities if they had no suburbs,' wrote the dramatist and pamphleteer Thomas Decker (*Lanthorne and Candlelight*, 1608),' 'sithence they serve but as caves, and monsters are bred up in them to devour the cities themselves.' By 1635 it was so taken for granted that cities had suburbs that the poet Francis Quarles endowed heaven with them in the shape of stars in his book *Emblems*: 'To heaven's high city I direct my journey,/ Whose spangled suburbs entertain my eye'.

Almost a century later, Daniel Defoe's *A Tour Thro' the Whole Island of Great Britain* (1726) began and ended in London; he symbolically placed his 50-page chapter on the city at the centre of the book. From Camberwell could be seen 'a fair prospect of the whole city of London itself; the most glorious sight without exception that the whole world at present can show.' Closer to, London is revealed as a shapeless sprawl.

> It is the disaster of London, as to the beauty of its figure, that it is thus stretched out in buildings, just at the pleasure of every builder, or undertaker of buildings, and as the convenience of the people directs, whether for trade, or otherwise; and this has spread the face of it in a most straggling, confus'd manner, out of all shape, uncompact, and unequal; neither long or broad, round or square; whereas the city of Rome, though a monster for its greatness, yet was, in a manner, round, with very few irregularities in its shape.

The arrival of railways speeded up London's growth exponentially, and the suburbs spread like dry rot. In *The Three Clerks* (1858) Anthony Trollope wrote, 'It is very difficult nowadays to say where the suburbs of London come to an end and where the country begins. The railways, instead of enabling Londoners to live in the country, have turned the country into a city. London will soon assume the shape of a great starfish. The old town, extending from Poplar to Hammersmith, will be the nucleus, and the various railway lines will be the projecting rays.'

As cities themselves grew enormous and dangerous, suburbs began to be seen as idyllic retreats, beloved by retired colonials who built themselves spacious bungalows in the leafy outskirts of busy conurbations. In *News From Nowhere* (1890), William Morris imagined the suburbs becoming a social utopia, that would be in sharp contrast to the grimy city fringes he glimpsed from his train window as he went home. Ebenezer Howard's *Garden Cities of Tomorrow* (1898) provided a practical script for its achievement.

Yet there remained a sense of second-best about suburbs; they were places for those out of the charmed circle of fashion, and those who could afford nothing better. George and Weedon Grossmith set the literary tone, describing the suburb as snug but anxiety-inducing in *Diary of a Nobody* (1892), their affectionate satire on lower-middle-class life in London's unfashionable margins. The Laurels, the Pooters' pretentiously named house in Brickfield Terrace, Upper Holloway, is 'a six-roomed residence, not counting basement, with a front breakfast-parlour', and a 'nice little garden that runs down to the railway'. Charles Pooter is a city clerk but one who, as he haughtily tells a belligerent tradesman, 'hopes he is also a gentleman', proud to be buying a 'cottage-piano on the three years' system'. The endearingly self-important Charles and his feather-headed wife Carrie, their jovial bachelor friends Cummings and Gowing, and Lupin – a Victorian 'Kevin', forever getting into scrapes – have become synonymous with suburban complacency.

No writer made more of the material and geographical surroundings of his characters than Arnold Bennett, celebrated for his novels about the 'Five Towns' of the Staffordshire potteries. He moved to London when a young man and developed a very early interest in the suburbs. His first novel, *A Man from the North* (1898), contrasts the country-bred Adeline's contempt for suburbia with her uncle Mr Aked's belief (shared by Bennett himself) that 'the suburbs are ... full of interest for those who can see it. Walk along this very street on such a Sunday afternoon as today. The roofs form two horrible, converging straight lines I know, but beneath there is character, individuality, enough to make the greatest book ever written.'

Mr Aked asks Adeline's fiancé Richard to collaborate with him on a book called *Psychology of the Suburbs*. 'Each of the great suburban divisions has, for me at any rate, its own characteristics, its peculiar

14   *The Diary of a Nobody.*

entrance, which saves the servant the trouble of going up to the front door, thereby taking her from her work. We have a nice little back garden which runs down to the railway. We were rather

The Laurels.

afraid of the noise of the trains at first, but the landlord said we should not notice them after a bit, and took £2 off the rent. He was certainly right;

BEYOND · THE · CITY
The Idyl of a Suburb

CHAPTER I.

The New-Comers.

"IF you please, mum," said the voice of a domestic from somewhere round the angle of the door, "number three is moving in."

Two little old ladies, who were sitting at either side of a table, sprang to their feet with ejaculations of interest, and rushed to the window of the sitting-room.

"Take care, Monica dear," said one, shrouding herself in the lace curtains; "don't let them see us."

"No, no, Bertha; we must not give them reason to say that their neighbours are inquisitive. But I think that we are safe if we stand like this."

The open window looked out upon a sloping lawn,

moral physiognomy', he explains. 'Each of these divisions must be described in turn, not topographically of course, but the inner spirit, the soul of it.' The play of one suburb on another and on the central haunts 'is as regular and as orderly, as calculable, as the law of gravity itself'. Richard leaves Aked's house with his head spinning with ideas, and sees the station at Parsons Green in a romantic new light.

> From the elevated platform grass was visible through a gently falling mist. The curving rails stole away mysteriously into a general grayness, and the twilight, assuaging every crudity of the suburban landscape, gave an impression of vast spaces and perfect serenity ... A signal suddenly shone out in the distance; it might have been a lighthouse seen across unnumbered miles of calm ocean.

Sir Arthur Conan Doyle's novel *Beyond the City: The Idyl of a Suburb* (1892) portrays suburbia as reassuringly ordinary, yet full of life and modernity. Young couples on bicycles are seen 'flying along the beautiful smooth suburban roads'; New Women join the local branch of the Emancipation Guild, and husbands are relieved to return 'from the crowds of Throgmorton Street to the peaceful avenues of Norwood' and to find it possible 'to do one's duties amid the babel of the City, and yet to live beyond it.' In 1907 Keble Howard also enthusiastically emphasised the safe normality of suburban life in *The Smiths of Surbiton: A Novel Without a Plot*: 'All Surbiton was gay with wonderful window-boxes and bright sunblinds'.

A more common imaginative response to the suburbs, however, was to see life there as fraught with social anxiety, insecurity about gender roles and uneasiness about neighbours. In George Gissing's *The Whirlpool* (1897) the women of Pinner are drawn as idle, extravagant parasites and the men as corrupt or impotent; any sense of geographical community is absent. Harvey Rolfe and his talented violinist wife Alma declare money-obsessed London 'a ghastly whirlpool which roars over a bottomless pit' and move to Wales, where their son is born, only for Alma to become jaded after two years by her cultural isolation. The couple compromise on a newly-built house in Pinner, within easy reach of London's shops and concert halls but, 'as [Alma] put it in her amusing way, 'on the outer edge of the whirlpool'.

The city is dangerously close, however, and subtly subversive of community. Harvey has the disturbing sense that their still damp new house 'was a shelter, a camp ... Thousands of men, who sleep on the circumference of London, and go

167

each day to business, are practically strangers to the district nominally their home; ever ready to strike tent, as convenience bids, they can feel no interest in a vicinage which merely happens to house them for the time being.'

In the same year, Richard Marsh's manic horror fantasy *The Beetle* was published, initially outselling Bram Stoker's *Dracula*, which also appeared in 1897. Marsh transforms the seemingly safe and cosy suburban street into a defenceless world, threatened by a sexually rapacious polymorphic monster who preys equally assiduously upon men and women. The underlying message is again the grasping materialism of women and their carelessness of male needs. Both Gissing and Marsh were early examples of a misanthropic literature concerned with the aspirational greed of idle, suburban women; this was also touched on with vicious intensity in John Masefield's *The Street of Today* (1911).

Metroland

Planned suburbs became reality in the arty and bohemian communities of Bedford Park in west London and Dame Henrietta Barnett's Hampstead Garden Suburb. Their popularity and extent rocketed after the tentacles of the London Metropolitan Railway had probed into the deepest rural recesses of Middlesex, Hertfordshire and Buckinghamshire in the 1880s, with 'garden cities' springing up in Letchworth (1903),

168

RIGHT
September 1911 edition of *'The Homestead'. An illustrated ABC Residential Gazette'.* It was issued quarterly by the Great Central and Metropolitan Railway Company to encourage a sense of community and tempt new residents to the western suburbs of London.

OPPOSITE
Cover of the score of 'My Little Metro-Land Home', a song written in 1920 to extol the delights of the residential developments growing up along the Metropolitan line.

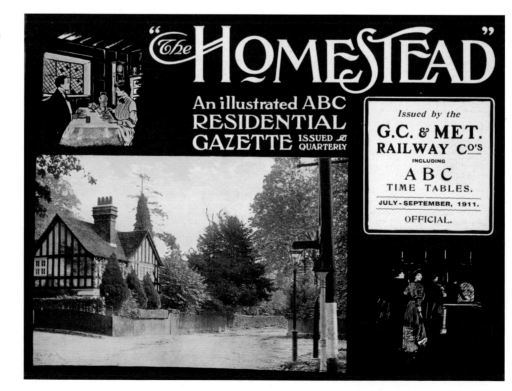

Hampstead (1907) and Welwyn (1917). The word 'Metro-Land' was coined in 1915 by James Garland, in-house copywriter to the 'Met'. 'Live in Metro-Land!' shouted slogans splashed across posters extolling the healthy and bracing air of Harrow Hill and Pinner; maps and guides showed places of interest near stations, including the inevitable golf courses. After the First World War, estates and new towns began to blight the idyllic orchards and fields shown in the railway carriage advertisements; in *Howards End* (1910), E.M. Forster deplores 'cosmopolitanism' and the reversion to 'the civilisation of luggage' represented by the new tendency to be constantly on the move. The encroachment of Metroland ('a verge in front of your house and grass and a tree for the dog') was only stopped in 1933 when London's cordon sanitaire, the 'Green Belt', was instituted.

Most people loved Metro-Land. Written in 1920, the jaunty song 'My Little Metro-Land Home' was thumped out on a thousand 'cottage-style' pianos; the name was borrowed for Triang's Tudor-style dolls' house. In R.C. Sherriff's *Greengates* (1936), retiring to Metroland is the fulfilment of the lives of the gentle protagonists. 'Bard of

Beaconsfield' John Betjeman (1906–84) was almost as fond of it as he was of Cornwall, celebrating it in such poems as 'The Metropolitan Railway' and 'Middlesex' from *A Few Late Chrysanthemums* (1954).

> Gaily into Ruislip Gardens
> Runs the red electric train,
> With a thousand Ta's and Pardon's
> Daintily alights Elaine;
> Hurries down the concrete station
> With a frown of concentration,
> Out into the outskirt's edges
> Where a few surviving hedges
> Keep alive our lost Elysium – rural Middlesex again.

In a 1973 BBC documentary Betjeman rode the line from the Baker Street station tearoom for suburban ladies past 'the serried avenues of Harrow's garden villages', seeking to discover how much the impossible dream of 'city man turned countryman' had turned into a nightmare of suburban sprawl. At Verney Junction, the last station, he turns to camera and says, 'The houses never got this far. Grass triumphs. And I must say I'm rather glad.'

Evelyn Waugh (1903–66) often poked fun at Betjeman, and satirised the suburbs in his novel *Decline and Fall* (1928). Its hero Pennyfeather's beloved Margot Beste-Chetwynde deserts him for the upwardly mobile but plebeian Viscount Metroland, Minister for Transportation. Metroland appears again in *Vile Bodies* (1930), this time complaisantly accepting his wife's adultery with the aristocratic Alistair Trumpington. Noblesse gets away with murder; the nouveau riche oblige.

Ambivalence prevails about childhoods spent in safe and prosperous suburban neighbourhoods. Some, such as John Osborne in his 1957 essay 'They Call It Cricket', John Fowles in his description of the pollarded but productive fruit trees in his father's suburban garden (*The Tree*, 1979) and Julian Barnes – whose first novel *Metroland* (1980) told of youthful aspiration and disillusion – experienced suburban childhoods as tedious, unaesthetic and unstimulating while also conceding that their very frustrations had a beneficial effect. At the beginning of *Metroland* Julian Barnes's fictional alter ego Christopher strolls the streets with a schoolfriend and complains about the orange glare of sodium lighting. 'They even fug up the spectrum', he complains. 'They' are 'the unidentified legislators, moralists, social luminaries and parents of outer suburbia'. But after tasting London and Paris, he retreats at the age of 30 into the married, mortgaged respectability of Metroland; sleepless one night, he reflects that the orange street lights make his pyjamas look brown; he too has become one of 'them'.

OPPOSITE
The tranquil opening of Katherine Mansfield's macabre *Suburban Fairy Tale*. First page of the original manuscript, 1919.

A Suburban Fairy Tale.

15. iii. 1919.

Mr and Mrs B. sat a breakfast in the cosy red
dining room of their 'snug little cot just under
half an hour's run from the city.'
There was a good fire in the grate — for the dining
room was the living room as well — the two
windows overlooking the cold empty garden patch
were closed, and the air smelled agreeably
of bacon and eggs, toast and coffee. Now that
this rationing business was, near, over Mr B. made a
point of a thoroughly good tuck in before facing
the very real perils of the day — He didn't mind
who knew it — he was a true Englishman
about his breakfast — he had to have it; he'd
carr on without it and if you told him that
these continental chaps could get through half
the mornings work he did on a role and
a coffee of coffee — you simply didn't know what
you were talking about. Mr B. was a stout

As the King paused a moment with his brush in his mouth, the Equerry announced Barker & Lambert. It did not surprise them to find His Majesty sitting on a floor littered with water-colour sketches for the excellent reason that the last time they had called he had been sitting on a floor littered with childrens' bricks and the time before that on a floor littered with wholly unsuccessful attempts to make a schoolboy's paper dart. They listened to his prattle as they would have done to that of a literal baby, Lambert with an idle grin and Barker with a face of adamant. Lambert cared for nothing but pleasure & found the King cheaper than a music hall. Barker cared for nothing but getting a certain number of state papers signed, & found the King always ready to do so, for signing his name, with a particular curl was one of his more enduring pleasures.

But today, when they had listened to the prattle for some minutes, something in the nature of the prattle alarmed them. So, sometimes, grown up people detect something in a child's monologue about fairyland which

175

LEFT
Pages from G.K. Chesterton's draft of *The Napoleon of Notting Hill*, a novel set in London in 1984, showing Chesterton's sketch of the baby owl-like Auberon Quin, who has been chosen by random selection to be the new King of England, talking to the vacuous civil servants James Barder and Wilfrid Lambert about his plans.

Suburban Dreaming

Ambivalence about suburban existence could easily slip into fantasising. The selfish complacency of suburbanites male and female was the theme of Katherine Mansfield's macabre short story 'A Suburban Fairy Tale' (1919). In this tale a couple discuss what they plan to eat over the next few days while their neglected son first gazes at an army of starving children (or are they sparrows?) outside the window and then disappears among them.

G.K. Chesterton (1874–1936) managed to create moments of rare menace as well as magic in his novel *The Napoleon of Notting Hill* (1904). 'I have never been to St John's Wood', declares his narrator. 'I dare not. I should be afraid of the innumerable night of the fir trees, afraid to come upon a blood red cup and the beating of the wings of the Eagle.' In his allegorical spy-thriller *The Man Who Was Thursday: A Nightmare* (1909), he parodied the highbrow separatism of the suburb of Bedford Park in his creation Saffron Park, which lies 'on the sunset side of London, as red and ragged as a cloud of sunset ... Its skyline was fantastic, and even its ground plan was wild ... It was described with some justice as an artistic colony, though it never in any definable way produced any art. But although its pretensions to be an intellectual centre were a little vague, its pretensions to be a pleasant place were quite indispensable.'

At nightfall, 'an attractive unreality fell upon it ... the little gardens were often illuminated, and the big Chinese lanterns glowed in the dwarfish trees like some fierce and monstrous fruit.' The novel opens at sunset on an evening when 'all the heaven seemed covered with a quite vivid and palpable plumage; you could only say that the sky was full of feathers'. Enter Gabriel Syme, apparently a poet, in fact an undercover policeman seeking to find out how real are the anarchistic pretensions of one of Saffron Park's residents, Lucian Gregory. Very real, it seems, when, after a debate on the poetical quality of railroad timetables, Gregory takes him to a Chiswick pub. There he operates a switch and the table at which they are sitting spins down into the earth; they find themselves in an underground arsenal, packed with guns and bombs. After a gasp-a-minute narrative of intrigues, disguises, horse chases, breaking windows and balloon escapes it emerges, however, that all the members of the cell into which Gregory introduces Syme are also undercover detectives, and

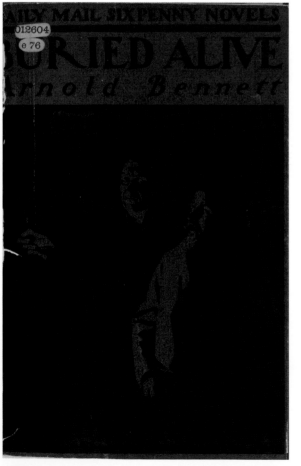

that they are led by no less a figure than the risen Christ. Syme swoons – only to wake again in Saffron Park, where birds hop and sing, and a pretty girl with red-gold hair is cutting lilacs before breakfast.

Arnold Bennett's wonderful comic tale *Buried Alive* (1908) showed how easily identity could be lost in the busy 'phantasmagoria' of Putney's Upper Richmond Road. No-one notices when Priam Farll, a famous but chronically shy artist, allows it to be assumed that he, rather than his valet, has died, and disappears into south London with a new wife much better at ministering to his creature comforts than his valet had ever been. Farll glories in the simplicity of Putney life, 'a place where you lived unvexed, untroubled' and which has its 'own splendours',

> There were theatre, music-hall, assembly-rooms, concert hall, market, brewery, library and an afternoon tea shop exactly like Regent Street; also churches and chapels; and Barnes Common if you walked one way, and Wimbledon Common if you walked another … Existence at Putney seemed to Priam Farll to approach the Utopian. It seemed to breathe of romance – the romance of common sense and kindliness and simplicity.

A rather nastier kind of romance is the theme of Jenny Diski's *Nothing Natural* (1986). Set in a flat in a north London suburb, Rachel embarks on a sado-masochistic relationship with a sinister man: the novel echoes the popular tabloid trope of illicit sexual practices taking place behind the net curtains of demure suburban houses. Crime writers have also found the anonymity of suburban lives ideal territory for interposing the murderous extraordinary into the ordinary – no longer a fantasy now that cars have become such convenient getaway vehicles for criminals. In Julian Symonds' *Something Like a Love Affair* (1992) Judith Lassiter feels that every morning she dons a mask of suburban mentality to fit the estate in which they live, 'a multitude of little red brick houses which differed only in minor details, in streets all named after flowers'; in fact she is plotting to kill her husband and escape with her lover. The protagonists of Minette Walters' *The Breaker* (1998) find themselves in a tree-lined suburban avenue in a south coast town, investigating the background of a victim from a council estate in the Midlands who had achieved her ambitions of 'a house of her own. Social acceptance. Respectability'. The murder in Colin Dexter's first Inspector Morse novel, *The Silent World of Nicholas Quinn* (1977), takes place in a north Oxford suburb; in later stories the contrast between the salubrious homes of Oxford dons and the deprived lives of those on Oxford's outer ring estates is repeatedly emphasised.

In Michael Frayn's *Spies* (2002) two schoolboys imagine that the quiet suburb in which they live is alive with German agents. The suburb is described as a 'sudden new colony'.

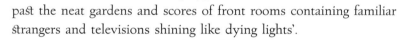

BELOW
Front cover of the first
paperback edition of
Hanif Kureishi's *The
Buddha of Suburbia*
(1990), a book which
humorously maps the
contrasting cultures
of different London
suburbs.

Muddy tracks were adopted and drained, tarred and gravelled, so that the wives could push their high-sprung perambulators to the shops without jolting their babies awake, and their husbands could walk dryshod in their city shoes to the station each morning and dryshod back at night. The raw earth and bare bricks of building plots were softened by a green screen that grew as Stephen grew.

The privet hedges signal hidden mysteries, things that must never be known. For J.K. Rowling it typifies both suburban normality and a veil of magical fantasy in *Harry Potter and the Philosopher's Stone* (1997). 'Mr. and Mrs. Dursley, of number four, Privet Drive, were proud to say that they were perfectly normal, thank you very much. They were the last people you'd expect to be involved in anything strange or mysterious.' And so it all began.

Hanif Kureishi's *The Buddha of Suburbia* (1990) is a suburban *Pilgrim's Progress*, the story of a mixed-race teenager's struggle to 'locate himself as a new breed of Englishman'. It is set in the 1970s – years of punk rock and alternative hippie culture, and the battle between the unions and the Conservative government that culminated in Thatcherism. 'My name is Karim Amir, and I am English born and bred, almost', runs its opening line. Teenage Karim despises his Bromley birthplace for its racial bigotry, genteel pretensions and arid public places. He walks to the pub with his friends 'past turdy parks, past the Victorian school with outside toilets, past the numerous bomb sites which were our true playgrounds and sexual schools, and

past the neat gardens and scores of front rooms containing familiar strangers and televisions shining like dying lights'.

Surveying the suburbs almost like an estate agent, Kureishi accurately calibrates the greater attractions of bay-windowed Beckenham and oak-shaded Chislehurst and the considerably lesser ones of grotty, neo-fascist Penge, before taking his hero nearer London's centre in the second part of the book. Karim moves to Barons Court, a colourful world in which 'there are thousands of black people everywhere' and 'kids in velvet cloaks who lived free lives' play The Doors on keyboards and beat bongo drums in Hyde Park. 'So this was London at last, and nothing gave me more pleasure than strolling round my new possessions all day.' He auditions for a Chelsea theatre company, getting the part of Mowgli despite the director finding him disappointingly suburban, with no romantic stories to tell about his Oriental background. In this cosmopolitan world he meets a Trotskyite Welshman from Brixton and rich, classy Eleanor who lives in Ladbroke Grove – an area 'that was slowly being reconstituted by the rich, but where Rasta dope-dealers still hung around outside pubs'. The zenith of his geographical and cultural pilgrimage is 'Brainyville', as he calls St John's Wood, but he is disappointed by the insincerity of the high Bohemian élite. The novel was originally called *The Streets of My Heart*, a title which may be less catchy but matches its message exactly.

J.G. Ballard (1930–2009), the 'Seer of Shepperton', had an obsession with dystopian man-made landscapes, and the psychological effect they have on their inhabitants. His science fiction writing and such books as *Crash* (1973) and *Concrete Island* (1974) may be sublimations of the horrors he witnessed as a child in Japanese prisoner-of-war camps; his attitude to life was made the blacker by the sudden death of his wife while they were on holiday with their children. Evidently a model father with, in later life, the benign aspect of a teddy bear, his imagination runs riot as he describes how the hyper-reality of the suburban non-space provokes murderously bizarre behaviour from inhabitants who have become devoid of emotion.

In the cautionary and sexually explicit *Crash* Ballard uses the car, source of more deaths and injuries than any pandemic cataclysm, 'as a total metaphor for man's life in society'. Equally obsessed with the penetrative damage caused by crashing cars and a desire to penetrate celebrities, Dr Robert Vaughan, 'former TV-scientist, turned nightmare angel of the expressways', practices on random victims his dream end-game: dying in a head-on collision while violating the iconic film actress Elizabeth Taylor. 'I wanted to rub the human face in its own vomit and force it to look itself in a mirror', wrote Ballard. *Concrete Island* is a twisted Robinson Crusoe, in which a man is marooned on a road island in the middle of a multi-layered road junction after a crash, and only suffers more injuries from oblivious passing cars when he tries to leave it. 'The whole city was now asleep, part of an immense, unconscious Europe, while he himself crawled about on a forgotten traffic island like the nightmare of this slumbering continent.'

Ballard succeeded in exorcising his demons with his two autobiographical novels, *Empire of the Sun* (1984) and *The Kindness of Women* (1991). But he returned to his view of suburbs as dystopic in his last novel, *Kingdom Come* (2006). 'The suburbs dream of violence', it begins, going on to examine the relationship between consumerism and fascism, and the way that advertising subverts morality. 'Mad is bad. Bad is good', runs a slogan for a microcar. A psychiatric patient on day release sprays the Brooklands Metro-Centre, an M25 shopping mall, with a machine gun, killing among others the father of retired pilot Stuart Pearson. But when Pearson tries to find out more about what happened, he finds himself preyed upon by thugs. The gated community in which his father lived is not what it seems; a 'suburban Dr Goebbels' is preparing to take over.

ABOVE
J.G. Ballard had an obsession with dystopian man-made landscapes: photograph taken in the 1970s by Fay Godwin.

machine sprung from a trap. An hour later
at his body under the police arc-lights.
The postures of his legs and arms, and the
his face, to the soft palate reminded me of the
wounds he had collected in the photographs of
crash injuries, that covered the walls of apartment. I looked
down at his Enlarged with blood, his jeans had become
inflated to twice its erect size. yards away, the film
actress stood below the revolving light, trembling on the arm
of her chauffeur whinnying before a dead
Vaughan had died at the moment of orgasm.
Before this Vaughan had been involved in many crashes.
I think of Vaughan now two months earlier at
the foot of the flyover, in a rehearsal of his own death. A young
man and woman were being helped from their car by
My first sight of
Vaughan was through the fractured windshield of the heavy saloon
car. His white face, with its eyes and slack mouth,
was lit by broken rainbows. I pulled the dented door
frame. He sat motionlessly on the broad seat, hands at his
sides covered with blood from his injured kneecaps. Vomit stained
the lapels of his leather jacket,
to the semen splashed across the steering column and
instrument panel. buttocks were clamped together
as if they had seized while the last drop from his vesicles.
Before he would allow me to move him
the zip of his trousers. Scattered on the floor beside him
were the photographs of the death-crashes and
James Dean which I had reproduced for him that morning at my
office.
For Vaughan the car-crash and his own sexuality had
a final marriage, the logic of strange eroticism which
carried him to his death over the railing of the flyover.
I remember him with the in
the crushed rear compartments of wrecked cars in
and the photographs of these young women in the
postures of their tight faces and uncomfortable
thighs lit up by his polaroid flash like the startled
survivors of submarine disaster. These strange young women,
cousins of the in the gallery of crash injury
photographs which Vaughan collected. Vaughan was fascinated
by the buboes of gas bacillus infections that ballooned in
bubbles on the legs of young women, facial

Musing on the Margins
In the land of lobelias and tennis flannels
The rabbit shall burrow and the thorn revisit,
The nettle shall flourish on the gravel court
And the wind shall say: 'Here were godless people:
Their only monument the asphalt road
And a thousand lost golf balls.
(T.S. Eliot, *The Rock*)

For centuries writers and poets have found Britain's furthest reaches inspirational. R.S. Thomas on the Lleyn Peninsula, George Mackay Brown in the Orkneys and Alistair MacLean in Ardnamurchan are the modern inheritors of an ancient tradition of seeking peace to cogitate, contemplate, and create word magic well away from civilisation's wheel-beaten tarmac. Cities also have remote corners, strange 'places in-between', that have inspired poetry. Philip Larkin, who worked for most of his life in Hull's University Library, evoked the city's cul-de-sac quality and the remoteness of its environs dryly yet affectionately in his poem 'Here':

… And out beyond its mortgaged, half-built edges
Fast-shadowed wheat-fields, running high as hedges,
Isolate villages, where removed lives
Loneliness clarifies. Here silence stands
Like heat. Here leaves unnoticed thicken,
Hidden weeds flower, neglected waters quicken …

In 1933 George Orwell wrote a poem about a wasteland near Hayes, on London's western fringes, called 'On a Ruined Farm near the His Master's Voice Gramophone Factory'. It describes how the poet looks one way at the 'factory towers, white and clear/Like distant, glittering cities' and the other at 'the black and budless trees,/The empty sties, the barns that stand/Like tumbling skeletons'. Unable to move or choose, he stands 'Between two countries, both-ways torn,/And moveless still, like Buridan's donkey/Between the water and the corn.' Britain as an island has, he implies, always been similarly Janus-faced, looking both out to sea and into its rural heartlands, poised between past and present, and its writers have revelled in exploring the tension of the contrast between land and sea, security and the unknown, limitations and potential.

The countryside campaigner Marion Shoard (b.1949) coined the word 'edgeland' for what she called 'the interfacial interzone between the urban and rural'. Poets Paul Farley and Michael Symmons Roberts took the idea and ran with it in *Edgelands: Journeys into England's True Wilderness* (2011). Remembering their childhoods in Liverpool

181

OPPOSITE
'I wanted to rub the human face in its own vomit'. Typescript of J.G. Ballard's *Crash* (1970–71) describing a collision engineered by the obsessed 'nightmare angel of the expressways', Robert Vaughan.

and Manchester, and the way they never quite reached the 'sunlit uplands of jigsaw puzzles and Ladybird books', however far they walked from the city, they made a series of excursions – north, south, east and west – into the spaces on the edges where urban and suburban order ends. In language that sings and inspires, Farley and Roberts salute paths that are unofficial, hideouts in sooty laurels, lonely canals, the ramshackle pigeon lofts of northern back gardens and the pallet's architectural potential. Boundaries are porous, pregnant with opportunity. 'Somewhere in the hollows and spaces between our carefully managed wilderness areas and the creeping, flattening effects of global capitalism, there are still places where an overlooked England truly exists … complicated, unexamined places that thrive on disregard, if we could only put aside our nostalgia for places we've never really known and see them afresh.' Walks with the dog need never be the same again.

In its introduction *Edgelands* pays homage to Richard Mabey (b.1941). A scientist with a sharp eye for the romantic, Mabey has been observing and recording the natural world's relation to human beings for almost forty years. *Flora Britannica* (1996) and *Birds Britannica* (2005) are both encyclopaedic and engagingly approachable, presenting places as vividly as their avian and vegetable occupants.

Mabey's first book, *Food for Free* (1972), a guide to plants that are both palatable and easily recognisable, became an instant best-seller. The year after he wrote it he published *The Unofficial Countryside* (1973), an appreciation of the natural beauties, varied wildlife and edible treasure trove of 'urban nature' that is discoverable on the despised margins of cities and industrial conglomerations. It was decades ahead of its time in celebrating nature's inherent toughness, its adaptability and its capacity

183

for improvised survival. A stone curlew is found curled up in a children's sandpit in Kilburn, while spotted orchids flourish in a wrecked car. Sunflowers loom at landfill sites, strayed growths from suburban budgies' seed mixes that ended up in dustbins. In the first summer after the Blitz rosebay willow herb flourished on over three-quarters of the bombed sites in London, providing 'defiant sparks amongst the desolation'. There are threats too in this burgeoning landscape: giant hogweed, thorn-apples and tumbleweed are invading unchecked.

Iain Sinclair, who introduced a new edition of the book in 2010, describes Mabey as 'the unacknowledged pivot' between the new school of nature writers – W.G. Sebald, Ronald Blythe, Roger Deakin, Robert Macfarlane – and 'those others, of a grungier disposition, who are randomly (and misleadingly) herded together as "psychogeographers"' (among them, he might have added, himself, Will Self and Peter Ackroyd). He was astonished, he writes, to find 'how accurately *The Unofficial Countryside* plotted my own future books'. Besides following, as Mabey did, in the footsteps of John Clare, Sinclair has for the last ten years increasingly interested himself in the outer edges of cities, literally and literarily circling the capital with *London Orbital: A Walk around the M25* (2002). 'Encircling London like a noose, the M25 is a road to nowhere', he reflects. This 'grim necklace' is 'the point where London loses it, gives up its ghosts'. Sinclair brings the districts bisected by the never-ending band of tarmac to life with pyrotechnic brilliance, weaving together modern reality, history, literature and legend to make a somewhere out of a nowhere, a respected entity out of a dreaded treadmill, excavating by his pedestrian progress the 'true territory for a fiction of England'.

BIBLIOGRAPHY

Ackroyd, Peter, *Albion: The Origins of the English Imagination*,
Chatto & Windus, 2002

Drabble, Margaret, *A Writer's Britain: Landscape in Literature*,
Thames & Hudson, 1994

Hahn, Daniel, & Robins, Nicholas, *The Oxford Guide to Literary Britain & Ireland*,
3rd edition, OUP, 2008

Hardyment, Christina, *Literary Trails: Writers in their Landscapes*,
National Trust, 2000

Hill, Susan, & Dudgeon, Piers, *The Spirit of Britain: an Illustrated Guide to Literary Britain*,
Headline, 1994

Schama, Simon, *Landscape and Memory*,
Harper Collins, 1995

Tindall, Gillian, *Countries of the Mind: The Meaning of Place to Writers*,
Hogarth Press, 1991

Sinclair, Iain, *London, City of Disappearances*,
Hamish Hamilton, 2006

Vansittart, Peter, *London: A Literary Companion*,
John Murray, 1992

Varlow, Sally, *A Reader's Guide to Writers' Britain*,
Prion, 1994

PICTURE CREDITS

11 © The Estate of Laurie Lee; 12 BL 12430.
dd.15; 13 BL C.38.f.28; 14 BL 12827.h.1/3; 15 BL
Add. Ms. 59678, f.35; 16 BL Cotton Ms. Nero
A.X., f.94v; 19 BL File 338; 20 BL C.123, f.2;
23 BL 11656.e.32 © The Estate of Agnes Miller
Parker; 24 Imperial War Museum, London;
25 © The Estate of Laurie Lee; 26 BL Add.
Ms. 88936/2/24, f.1. Reprinted by permission
of United Agents on behalf of the Estate of
Laurie Lee; 38 BL Ac.9490/31; 29 The British
Museum, London; 30 BL W9/8284; 31 BL
012808.dd.41; 32 BL NN.16795 © The Estate of
Norman Hepple; 33 BL Add. Ms. 56351B, f.2.
Reproduced with permission of Curtis Brown
Group Ltd., London on behalf of the Estate of
Stella Gibbons. Copyright © Stella Gibbons,
1932; 36 BL Ashley 3270; 38 BL Add. Ms.
37538F; 40 Stevenage Museum; 41 © David
Newham/Alamy; 42 Science Museum/Science
& Society Picture Library; 45 BL 650.b.23; 46
BL C.190.c.12; 49 BL Add. Ms. 34036, f.193; 50
BL N.2138; 51–52 BL Add. Ms. 61971, ff.28v-29;
55 The British Museum, London; 56 Pictorial
Press Ltd./Alamy; 57 BL Add. Ms. 46129, f.2;
58 BL 7105.e.21; 60 20th Century Fox/The
Kobal Collection; 61 BL AAD/1995/8/19/307.
Photo V&A Images; 62 BL 010352.c.39; 63 BL
Add. Ms. 73083, f.234; 65 Woodfall/British
Lion/The Kobal Collection; 68 BL Add. Ms.
53772, f.145v. © The Estate of W. H. Auden.
Reprinted by permission of Curtis Brown,
Ltd.; 71 BL FG1132-6-3; 72 BL Cup.652.c.5;
75 BL Cup.410.g.425; 76 Private Collection/
The Bridgeman Art Library; 77 BL Maps
K.Top.31.16.g.2; 78 BL 191.g.20; 80 BL Add. Ms.
47494, f.4r; 82 BL Add. Ms. 47864, f.80; 84 BL
Maps K.Top.50.82; 85 BL 83.k.2; 87 BL FG3017-
1; 88 BL Add. Ms. 43474, f.185; 91 BL Add.
Ms. 88918/1/23 © The Estate of Ted Hughes; 92
photo1st/istock-photo.com; 94 BL Cup.410.g.74;
96 The British Museum, London; 98 BL
C.194.b.199; 99 BL C.194.b.116; 100 BL 1502/320;

102 Associated British/The Kobal Collection;
104 Private Collection/Charles Plante Fine
Arts/The Bridgeman Art Library; 106 BL
AAD/1995/8/3236. Photo V&A Images; 107
© David Croucher/Alamy; 108 BL Add. Ms.
88919/4/1 © Graham Swift; 109 BL 10354.aa.14.
(24); 111 BL 12802.d.9; 112 BL C.131.c.7; 114 BL
C.105, f.3; 115 BL Add. Ms. 50855, f.4; 117 BL
AAD/1995/9/103/440. Photo V&A Images; 118 ©
Paul Glendell/Alamy; 120 BL C.186.bb.18; 123
BL 012632.i.2; 124 BL 10353.d.11. © The Estate
of Robert Gibbings; 126–127 BL 648.c.16; 128
Mary Evans Picture Library/Alamy; 129 BL
H.95/3648; 130 BL C.194.b.305-307; 132–133
BL Sloane Ms. 2596, f.5; 134 BL Lansdowne
Ms. 851, f.2; 135 BL Add. Ms. 35157, f.25; 136
BL Harley Ms. 7334, f.1; 137 The British
Museum, London; 138 BL C.194.b.305-307; 140
BL Wf1/1856; 141 BL Add. Ms. 49460, f.56r;
142 BL C.7.d.19; 144 BL C.194.b.305-307; 145
BL G.18068; 147 BL 11770.bb.4; 148 BL 012603.
bb.29; 150 BL Tab.700.b.3; 152 BL 12352.r.26;
155 BL Add. Ms. 51045, f.5; 156 BL Add. Ms.
88899/1/17.© The Estate of Angela Carter; 158
© John Bowling/Alamy; 159 BL X907/6454. ©
The Estate of B.S. Johnson; 160 Bert Hardy/
Picture Post/Getty Images; 162 BL Add. Ms.
88938/3/23/1. © J.G. Ballard. Reproduced by
permission. All rights reserved; 165 BL 012314,
f.25; 166 BL 012630.e.13; 167 BL 012625.k.14; 168
BL PP.2500.arb; 169 BL VOC/1920/Thraile;
170 Mark Kauffman/Time Life Pictures/Getty
Images; 171 BL Add.Ms. 71956B, ff.6v-7r. ©
John Betjeman by permission of the Estate of
John Betjeman; 173 BL Add. Ms. 612128, f.1;
174–175 BL Add. Ms. 73353F, f.1v-2r; 176 BL
012604.e.1/78; 178 BL H.91/1533; 179 BL FG2744-
3-14a; 180 BL Add. Ms. 88938/3/8, f.2. © J.G.
Ballard. Reproduced by permission. All rights
reserved; 182 BL FG226-331a-3; 183 BH Generic
Stock Images/Alamy.

INDEX

189

To my Grandchildren, in the hope that they too
will become literary explorers

Acknowledgements

This book would have been impossible to put together without the rich and inspiring input of Jamie Andrews, Janet Benoy, Rachel Foss and Tanya Kirk, the four curators of the British Library's exhibition, *Writing Britain: Wastelands to Wonderlands,* which it is intended to complement and memorialise. Although necessarily shaped by the topics to be featured in the exhibition, the book's narrative is, with all faults, my own, and I touch on numerous things that do not appear in the exhibition. Sally Nicholls has done wonders in finding illustrations to suit it, and Lara Speicher has been the most sensitive and encouraging of editors. As always, the London Library performed miracles with its lightning parcel post service to their most demanding country member. I am indebted to Peter Snow for some thoughtful initial input, and my wonderfully forebearing family, from whom I remained immured for several months. I dedicate the book to my six (and subsequent) grandchildren, in the hope that they will find in it treasure trove.

First published in 2012 by
The British Library, 96 Euston Road, London NW1 2DB

On the occasion of the exhibition
Writing Britain: Wastelands to Wonderlands
11 May–25 September 2012

Text © Christina Hardyment 2012
Images © 2012 The British Library
and other named copyright holders

British Library Cataloguing-in-Publication Data
A catalogue record is available from The British Library
ISBN 978-0-7123-5874-3 (hardback)
ISBN 978-0-7123-5875-0 (paperback)

Designed and typeset by Andrew Barron, thextension
Printed and bound in Italy by Printer Trento S.r.l

HALF-TITLE PAGE
Map by Stephen Spurrier for *Swallows and Amazons* by Arthur Ransome.

FRONTISPIECE
Illustration by Arthur Rackham for *The Wind in the Willows* (1940).

PAGE 4
Bartholomew Fair, London.
Aquatint from *Microcosm of London* (1808–10).

PAGES 6–7
Heptonstall, Yorkshire (1971), by Fay Godwin for Ted Hughes's *Remains of Elmet*.